U0732518

中国金融部门评估规划系列报告

中国金融部门评估报告

CHINA FINANCIAL SECTOR ASSESSMENT

世界银行 编著 　　 中国人民银行 译

中国金融出版社

责任编辑：戴　硕　董　飞
责任校对：孙　蕊
责任印制：程　颖

图书在版编目（CIP）数据

中国金融部门评估报告（Zhongguo Jinrong Bumen Pinggu Baogao）/世界银行编著；中国人民银行译 . —北京：中国金融出版社，2012.7
（中国金融部门评估规划系列报告）
ISBN 978 - 7 - 5049 - 6345 - 1

Ⅰ.①中⋯　Ⅱ.①世⋯②中⋯　Ⅲ.①金融事业—经济发展—研究报告—中国
Ⅳ.①F832

中国版本图书馆 CIP 数据核字（2012）第 063135 号

出版
发行　中国金融出版社

社址　北京市丰台区益泽路 2 号
市场开发部　（010）63266347，63805472，63439533（传真）
网上书店　http：//www.chinafph.com　（010）63286832，63365686（传真）
读者服务部　（010）66070833，62568380
邮编　100071
经销　新华书店
印刷　北京市松源印刷有限公司
尺寸　185 毫米×260 毫米
印张　5.75
字数　84 千
版次　2012 年 7 月第 1 版
印次　2012 年 7 月第 1 次印刷
定价　15.00 元
ISBN 978 - 7 - 5049 - 6345 - 1/F.5905
如出现印装错误本社负责调换　联系电话　（010）63263947

《中国金融部门评估规划系列报告》总序

亚洲金融危机之后，国际货币基金组织和世界银行联合推出金融部门评估规划（FSAP），致力于全面、客观地评估成员经济体金融体系的稳健状况，减少金融危机发生的可能性，并推动金融改革和发展。此次国际金融危机进一步凸显评估工作的重要性，二十国集团（G20）领导人在华盛顿和伦敦峰会上两次承诺将对本国进行FSAP评估。国际货币基金组织认真总结FSAP推出十年来的经验，并结合危机教训，进一步完善FSAP评估框架和评估方法，更加关注系统性风险、跨境溢出效应和危机管理框架等，重点评估对象也由新兴市场经济体转向了系统重要性国家和金融中心，针对性和有效性得到了进一步提升，逐渐成为国际社会广泛接受的评估机制。

中国金融管理部门一贯重视金融稳定监测与评估。早在2003年初，人民银行就牵头相关部门组成了跨部门小组，用一年多时间对我国金融体系的稳定状况开展了系统的自评估。这对于我们摸清家底、防范和化解金融风险、维护金融稳定起到了积极作用。2005年开始，人民银行定期发布《中国金融稳定报告》，在日常监测各类风险的基础上，全面分析、评估金融体系的稳健性状况。各行业监管部门也进一步加强了对相关金融行业风险状况的及时监测和评估。

与此同时，中国政府坚定不移地推进金融领域的改革，以改革促进金融业的发展和稳定。特别是2003年以来，抓住我国经济平稳较快增长的战略机遇期，果断推进和完成了主要大型金融机构财务重组、引进战略投资者、公开上市等一系列具有里程碑意义的重大金融改革。随着改革的深入，我国金融业的整体面貌发生了历史性变化，大型金融机构财务状况有了根本的好转，公司治理不断规范，抗风险能力显著提升，金融业整体实力持续增强，成功经受住了此次国际金融危机的严峻考验。在此过程中，中国金融业和金融市场实施相关国际标准的程度不断得到提升，为接受国际组织的全面评估奠定了良好基础。

在这样一种情况下，我们适时把握国际国内经济金融的最佳时机，在2009年8月启动了中国首次FSAP评估。为保障评估工作顺利进行，人民银行会同11个部门成立FSAP部际领导小组和部际工作小组，建立了相应的工作机制和工作原则。各成员单位高度重视FSAP评估，抽调精干力量，认真开展各项工作。经过人民银行和有关部门以及评估团历时两年多的精心组织和努力工作，评估于2011年11月圆满完成。随后，人民银行和国际货币基金组织在上海联合举办了"金融稳定监测与管理：来自 FSAP 的经验和改进 FSAP 的建议"国际研讨会，邀请 17 个亚太国家（地区）金融管理部门和主要国际金融组织的高层代表，以及美、英等一些国家驻基金组织执行董事，分享中国 FSAP 的成功经验，交流国际金融稳定评估的有效做法，以此促进金融稳定监测和管理的国际合作。

此次 FSAP 是中国金融体系首次接受国际组织进行第三方独立评估，实际上是从国际视角对我国金融体系和制度框架进行了一次全面"体检"，可以作为我国金融稳定自评估的重要补充。在符合我国有关法律法规和保密要求的前提下，我方向评估团提供了近百万字 FSAP 问卷答复材料，与其进行了 400 余场会谈，使其对我国金融体系有了更加深入、客观的认识和理解。评估团在此基础上撰写了一系列评估报告，充分肯定了中国金融业改革、发展和维护稳定的成就。报告认为，得益于中国政府推出的多项重大金融改革以及中央银行和各监管部门的有效监管，中国金融体系整体稳定，金融改革进展良好，金融机构实力不断增强，金融服务和产品日益多样化，有力支持了经济发展。

与此同时，评估报告也指出了我国金融体系的潜在风险，并就中国金融改革和发展提出了很多值得借鉴的建议。其中大部分建议，例如推进利率市场化改革、加强金融监管协调、构建逆周期宏观审慎制度框架等，在我国的"十二五"规划中已有明确表述；在 2012 年年初召开的全国金融工作会议上也得到了进一步强调。这说明，中外双方关于推进中国金融改革、维护金融稳定的很多观点是基本一致的。在明确改革方向的同时，作为发展中国家和经济转型国家，我们在学习借鉴国际经验做法的同时，有必要结合中国的具体国情以及国内金融业的特点，以我为主，因地制宜，在具体推进改革步骤时保持灵活性。下一步，在落实"十二五"规划和全国金融工作会议精神的过程中，我们要加快重点领域和关键环节改革，继续加强和改进金融宏观调控，推进利率和汇率改革，加快多层次金融市场体系建设，深化金融机构改革，推动存款保险制度建设，提升金融稳定和危机管理框架，进一步提高金融服务质量和效率。

FSAP 评估是一项持续性工作。作为具有全球系统重要性金融体系的 25 个国家（地区）之一，中国今后将每五年开展一次 FSAP 更新评估。同时，将 FSAP 建议的采纳及落实情况纳入"基金组织第四条款年度磋商"范畴，并在每次评估两年后就建议落实情况接受金融稳定理事会"国家同行评估"。我们愿在此基础上加深与国际金融组织的合作与交流，借鉴国际组织的良好做法，完善自身金融稳定评估框架，提升遵守国际标准与准则的程度。同时，积极参与全球经济金融治理改革，主动参与国际金融标准与准则的制定和修订，增强标准与准则的适用性和公平性。

在中国首次 FSAP 圆满完成后，人民银行会同银监会、证监会和保监会将中国 FSAP 系列报告翻译出版。在此，我对外方评估团专家和中方参与 FSAP 的各部门领导和工作人员、业界专家、学者表示衷心的感谢与敬意，他们以杰出的专业精神为中国 FSAP 付出了辛勤努力。希望这套系列报告能够及时介绍国际金融组织对中国金融改革和发展的评估结论，为金融管理部门和业界人士、以及关心中国金融改革和发展的专家、学者深入研究和借鉴 FSAP 评估建议提供参考，为进一步提升中国金融体系的稳健性作出积极贡献。

周小川

2012 年 6 月 26 日

中国金融部门评估规划部际领导小组

组　长：中国人民银行行长　　　　　　　　　周小川

副组长：中国人民银行副行长　　　　　　　　刘士余

成　员：外交部副部长　　　　　　　　　　　崔天凯

　　　　国家发展和改革委员会副主任　　　　朱之鑫

　　　　财政部副部长　　　　　　　　　　　李　勇

　　　　人力资源和社会保障部副部长　　　　胡晓义

　　　　商务部部长助理　　　　　　　　　　李荣灿

　　　　国家统计局副局长　　　　　　　　　许宪春

　　　　国务院法制办公室副主任　　　　　　安　建

　　　　银监会副主席　　　　　　　　　　　王兆星

　　　　证监会副主席　　　　　　　　　　　姚　刚

　　　　保监会副主席　　　　　　　　　　　李克穆

　　　　国家外汇管理局局长　　　　　　　　易　纲

中国金融部门评估规划部际工作小组

组　长：中国人民银行　　　　　　　宣昌能

副组长①：中国人民银行　　　　　　　梁世栋　黄晓龙

成　员：外交部　　　　　　　　　　李克新

　　　　国家发展和改革委员会　　　徐　林

　　　　财政部　　　　　　　　　　孙晓霞

　　　　人力资源和社会保障部　　　张　浩

　　　　商务部　　　　　　　　　　刘景嵩

　　　　中国人民银行　　　　　　　邵伏军　张晓慧　李　波　邢毓静

　　　　　　　　　　　　　　　　　张健华　金中夏　王　煜　刘争鸣

　　　　　　　　　　　　　　　　　万存知　李晓枫　刘　荣　孙　辉

　　　　　　　　　　　　　　　　　苟文均　边志良　霍颖励　阮健宏

　　　　　　　　　　　　　　　　　李　跃　周金黄　陆书春　朱　隽

　　　　　　　　　　　　　　　　　易　诚　王关荣

　　　　国家统计局　　　　　　　　董礼华

　　　　国务院法制办公室　　　　　刘长春

　　　　银监会　　　　　　　　　　刘春航　李文泓

　　　　证监会　　　　　　　　　　韩　萍

　　　　保监会　　　　　　　　　　姜　波

　　　　国家外汇管理局　　　　　　王允贵

---

① 金荦和孙平曾先后担任工作小组副组长并兼任工作小组办公室主任，在中国首次 FSAP 的不同阶段做了大量工作，目前已不再担任此职务。

中国金融部门评估规划部际工作小组办公室

主　任：梁世栋

副主任：王素珍

成　员：范智勇　王尊州　曲天石　那丽丽

　　　　陶　东　李敏波　林　毅　姚　斌

　　　　边永平　陈　蒂　余雪扬　冯　云

　　　　陈　岩　周正清　苏宏召　王　濛

《中国金融部门评估报告》

编审组： 刘士余　李　勇　王兆星　姚　刚　李克穆

执行组： 宣昌能　孙晓霞　刘春航　童道驰　姜　波

翻译组： 梁世栋　王素珍　曲天石　那丽丽　陈　苇

前　言

在总结 1997 年亚洲金融危机教训的基础上，国际货币基金组织和世界银行于 1999 年 5 月联合推出了"金融部门评估规划"（Financial Sector Assessment Program, FSAP），旨在通过金融稳健指标分析、压力测试和国际标准与准则评估等方法，加强对基金组织成员国（地区）金融脆弱性的监测与评估，减少金融危机发生的可能性，并推动成员国的金融改革和发展。经过不断发展和完善，FSAP 已成为国际社会广泛接受的金融稳定评估框架。截至 2011 年底，已有 130 多个国家（地区）完成了 FSAP 评估，许多国家（地区）还在初次评估的基础上进行了更新评估。

2008 年 2 月，温家宝总理在会见基金组织时任总裁时宣布中国将参加 FSAP 评估；此后，胡锦涛主席在二十国集团（G20）华盛顿峰会和伦敦峰会上两次做出接受 FSAP 评估的承诺。为落实我国承诺，从国际视角审视我国金融体系的稳健性，2009 年 8 月，我国正式接受国际货币基金组织和世界银行进行中国首次 FSAP 评估。中国人民银行会同外交部、发展改革委、财政部、人力资源和社会保障部、商务部、统计局、法制办、银监会、证监会、保监会、外汇局等 11 个部门成立了 FSAP 部际领导小组和部际工作小组，建立了相应的工作机制和工作原则，全力做好各项评估工作。

中国 FSAP 评估团由国际货币基金组织和世界银行的官员以及从其他国家聘请的财政部门、中央银行及银行、证券、保险等领域的专家组成。2010 年以来，评估团两次来华开展现场评估，部分成员多次来华进行专项评估和后续磋商，先后与国务院相关部门、部分地方政府、大型金融机构、中介机构等举行 400 余场会谈，就中国宏观金融风险和金融体系脆弱性、金融监管环境、金融体系流动性和金融稳定、金融市场基础设施建设、金融发展和金融服务可获得性、应急预案和危机管理安排等六方面内容展开深入交流。

经过两年多的努力，中国首次 FSAP 于 2011 年 11 月圆满完成。FSAP 评估团在中方提供的数据、信息、自评估报告和现场评估会谈的基础上撰写了一系列评估报告，主要包括《中国金融体系稳定评估报告》、《中国金融部门评估报告》、中国执行银行业、证券业、保险业、支付系统和证券结算系统等领域国际标准与准则情况的五份详细评估报告。上述报告对中国金融体系进行了系统、全面的评估，充分肯定了近年来我国金融改革和发展的巨大成就，对潜在的风险进行了提示，并提出了相应的改革建议。这些报告的英文版已在国际货币基金组织和世界银行的网站上公布。

  我们及时组织翻译出版这七份报告，以期通过介绍国际金融组织对中国金融体系稳定性的评估结论，为读者深入研究 FSAP 评估建议提供有益的参考。

中国 FSAP 部际工作小组办公室

2012 年 6 月 28 日

FSAP

金融部门评估规划

世界银行和国际货币基金组织联合倡议

2011年11月

本报告由世界银行评估人员撰写。世界银行不保证其中数据的准确性。报告中的发现、说明和结论未必反映世界银行执行董事及其代表的政府的观点。

目　　录

图

附表

缩略词表

AMC	资产管理公司
AML	反洗钱
AML/CFT	反洗钱/反恐融资
CAS	中国会计准则
CBRC	中国银监会
CCDC	中央国债登记结算有限责任公司
CCP	中央对手方
CFETS	中国外汇交易中心
CIRC	中国保监会
CNPS	中国支付清算体系
CSRC	中国证监会
DC	国内并表
EA	企业年金
FATF	反洗钱金融行动特别工作组
FHCs	金融控股公司
FI	金融中介
FSAP	金融部门评估规划
FX	外汇
GEB	创业板
HVPS	大额支付系统
IASB	国际会计准则委员会
IBBM	银行间债券市场
IFRS	国际财务报告准则
IOSCO	国际证监会组织
JSCBs	股份制商业银行
IPOs	首次公开上市
LCBs	大型商业银行
LGFP	地方政府融资平台
MCCs	小额贷款公司

MMMFs	货币市场基金
MOC	商务部
MOF	财政部
MSEs	小微企业
MTPL	机动车交通事故责任强制保险
NBS	国家统计局
NDRC	国家发展和改革委员会
NBFIs	非银行金融机构
NPLs	不良贷款
NSSF	全国社会保障基金
OFIs	其他金融机构
PBC	中国人民银行
PE	私募股权
PSBC	中国邮政储蓄银行
QFIIs	合格境外机构投资者
RBC	风险资本
RCCs	农村信用社
RMB	人民币（元）
SD&C	中国证券登记结算有限责任公司
SHFE	上海期货交易所
SIFIs	系统重要性金融机构
SIPS	系统重要性支付系统
SIVs	结构性投资工具
SSE	上海证券交易所
SME	中小企业
SOE	国有企业
SZSE	深圳证券交易所
WMC	理财公司
WMP	理财产品
WTO	世界贸易组织
VAT	增值税
VTB	村镇银行
ZCE	郑州商品交易所

摘　　要

本报告总结了 2010 年国际货币基金组织/世界银行联合评估团对中国开展金融部门评估规划（FSAP）的评估结论①。在第一次现场评估期间（2010 年 6 月），评估团对部分国际标准和准则的执行情况进行了评估，并就金融领域的许多议题展开了广泛的讨论；第二次现场评估（2010 年 12 月）完成了评估，并提交了《中国FSAP 备忘录》初稿以及一系列技术文本和背景文本初稿，这些评估报告涵盖了关于中国金融业的许多议题。

中国金融体系改革取得了积极成效。2003 年后，改革进一步加快，中国政府采取了一系列政策措施，增强金融体系弹性，优化金融结构，大力强化国内金融机构，增强市场信心。然而，风险、挑战和发展机遇并存。

本报告指出了随着金融部门现代化的继续，短期内中国所面临的风险、改革挑战和发展机遇。中国面临的潜在脆弱性、短期风险和政策诱发的扭曲现象，是发展中的金融体系的共同特征。这些挑战和机遇并非中国特有，是可以解决的。我们建议当局认真考虑以下改革发展顺序：（1）进一步加快金融体系商业化进程；（2）运用更加市场化的工具调控货币金融环境；（3）进一步加强监管；（4）增强金融稳定和危机管理框架；（5）完善普惠金融战略以改进金融服务可获得性；（6）继续支持资本市场发展；（7）继续加强和深化保险和养老金体系；（8）继续改进金融市场基础设施。

面对机遇和挑战，需要有创造性思维和变革的意愿。渐进的、分割的金融改革方式不能适应中国金融市场持续深化和复杂化的需要。因此，重要的是，要针对市场变化统筹考虑，在现有法律法规范畴之外探索可行方法，消除影响政府目标实现的障碍因素。

评估团与中国 FSAP 部际工作小组成员单位及其他部委和部门的高级官员和工

---

① 国际货币基金组织/世界银行中国 FSAP 评估团成员包括：Jonathan Fiechter（国际货币基金组织，评估团联席团长），Thomas A. Rose（世界银行，评估团联席团长），Udaibir S. Das（副团长，国际货币基金组织），Mario Guadamillas（副团长，世界银行），Massimo Cirasino, Patrick Conroy, Asli Demirgüç-Kunt, Catiana Garcia-Kilroy, Haocong Ren, Heinz Rudolph, Jun Wang, Ying Wang, Luan Zhao（均来自世界银行）；César Arias, Martin Čihák, Silvia Iorgova, Yinqiu Lu, Aditya Narain, Nathan Porter, Shaun Roache, Tao Sun, Murtaza Syed（均来自国际货币基金组织）；Nuno Cassola, Henning Göbel, Keith Hall, Nick Le Pan, Rodney Lester, Greg Tanzer, Nancy Wentzler, and Walter Yao（均为外部专家）。

3

作人员举行了会谈。中国 FSAP 部际工作小组成员单位包括外交部、国家发展和改革委员会、财政部、人力资源和社会保障部、商务部、中国人民银行、国家统计局、国务院法制办公室、银行业监督管理委员会、证券监督管理委员会、保险监督管理委员会和外汇管理局。其他部委和部门包括工业和信息化部、住房和城乡建设部、农业部、审计署、国有资产监督管理委员会、国家税务总局和全国社会保障基金理事会。评估团还在北京、重庆、广州、南昌、宁波、上海和深圳与金融机构和行业组织的代表以及私营部门代表举行了会谈。

评估团向中国当局及相关方面的热情接待、业务交流及慷慨支持表示衷心的感谢。

总体评估和建议

1. 中国金融体系改革进展良好。 当局正力求将金融部门从中央直接管理的体系转变为商业运作、财务健康的体系。金融体系的结构和运行状况正在改进，监管得到加强，透明度和开放度不断提高。

2. 中国正面临着潜在风险（包括更大的外部冲击风险）不断累积的挑战。 跨市场、跨机构联系日益增加，事实性的银行机构和非正规信贷市场、（金融）控股公司、表外业务呈上升趋势。农村中小金融机构改革正在继续。应密切监测、改进数据收集、加强信息共享并建立更有效的框架，以识别并解决问题机构以及那些可能影响当前改革进程的市场行为。

3. 短期国内风险包括四个方面： （1）近期信贷迅速扩张对银行资产质量的影响；（2）表外风险敞口的上升和正规银行部门以外贷款的增加；（3）房地产价格和大宗商品价格处于相对高位；（4）当前经济增长模式导致的失衡加剧。对17家主要商业银行开展的压力测试表明，大部分银行能够承受单个风险的冲击，但由于信息缺失问题，还不能确切评估这些风险通过经济金融体系的传导效应。如果所有这些风险同时发生，将会对金融稳定和改革产生不利影响。

4. 进一步协调经济政策和金融政策，以激励金融体系持续有效地向商业化转型。 重点是优化信贷资源配置、完善金融市场、改进金融服务，降低过高的预防性储蓄需求，并建立更具弹性、更加透明的制度框架。为顺利实现这一目标，政府必须继续调整其角色和职责。目前，政府通过行使对银行和国有企业所有权、利率管制、制定金融体系优先发展政策和提供隐性担保等行为参与金融市场和机构，引发了道德风险，弱化了银行风险管理，积累了或有风险和负债。

5. 要加快金融体系商业化进程。 信用风险战略由贷款增长目标主导。需要用其他机制来替代商业银行信贷在政府政策目标中的作用，包括直接财政支出、政府信贷项目、理顺政策性银行经营机制等。银行风险管理和监管评估过于注重历史变量，对前瞻性信用风险评估的重视程度不够。银行风险敞口高度集中于国有企业、保证利差、银行对贷款利率进行差别管理的能力和意愿不足，以及对信贷投放的隐性指导等，均削弱了银行对信用风险进行有效管理的动力。因此，运用更加市场化的方式来调控货币金融环境，将极大地改善信贷配置。管理信贷扩张的首要工具应该是市场利率。

6. 要持续改进监管制度。应努力实施并表监管，并确保在所有相关政府部门之间及时共享重要信息。人民银行和主要监管机构必须拥有与其日益增多的职责相一致的权力和资源。监管机构应重点确保被监管机构的安全性、稳健性和市场行为的适当性。在日常监管中，应采用更具前瞻性的监管方法，而不是发布大量监管规则和使用非常详细的审批程序。此外，应通过改善信息披露和加强金融教育等方式，提高金融消费者承担潜在风险和义务的意识。为此，需提高会计要求、数据标准、报告要求和信息披露要求。

7. 建立正式的金融稳定框架来监测并应对宏观金融脆弱性，将有利于中国今后的发展。根据 2008 年 6 月设立特别委员会的经验，应建立常设的金融稳定委员会，该委员会应有权获得有关监管信息和其他金融信息。

8. 需建立能够及时处置问题金融机构的框架。该框架应有助于以最小的社会成本处置问题金融机构，并实现问题金融机构的有序清算。为实现这一目标并保护中央银行资产负债表，可建立存款保险基金，为有序处置破产机构提供资金，并保护受保存款人。应授权一家政府部门监测金融体系的稳健性，并处置被监管者视为无法存续的金融机构。

9. 更加广泛且多样化的金融产品和服务将有助于深化和加强中国金融体系。应考虑政府与固定收益市场和利率政策之间的关系。这包括：（1）更积极地支持政府债券发行，完善无风险收益率曲线；（2）扩大非政府发行主体范围；（3）适度增加不同类型的金融工具，满足发行人和投资者的多样化需求。同时，还应完善回购市场，开发风险池和对冲产品，审慎推进资产证券化，确保对各种类型固定收益产品监管规则的一致性。

10. 金融基础设施和法律框架需进一步完善。成绩有目共睹，但尚需：（1）强化与支付系统和证券结算系统相关的法律框架和监督；（2）改善征信系统的覆盖范围和质量；（3）改进对信用评级机构的监管并提高评级质量；（4）完善并加强消费者保护；（5）强化破产机制和债权人权益；（6）明确问题金融机构的处置程序和对存款人的保护；（7）建立符合宏观审慎和金融稳定要求的框架和工具。

11. 完善政策以扩大金融覆盖范围。实施改革措施以提供如下正向激励机制：金融服务投向服务不足的领域；改善市场竞争力和竞争环境（通过调整准入和退出标准）；完善有关普惠金融的法律框架；废除与提高金融可获得性总体目标不一致的政策。

12. 确定合适的改革顺序和步骤富有挑战，但对中国经济持续增长十分关键。在使风险极小化的同时保持发展与金融稳定之间的平衡至关重要。为推动这一进程，附表 1 列出了需要考虑的主要建议的优先次序。

I. 金融体系结构和功能

A. 背景

1. 中国金融体系改革和发展取得了巨大成就（附表2）。这些成就得益于主要银行的改革、资本市场的创立、审慎监管制度的引入、银行注资、加入世界贸易组织后金融体系的对外开放以及2003年以后的改革举措。包括政府注资、引入战略投资者和公开上市在内的股份制改革，推动了大型银行的商业化转型。银行股权结构多元化，公司治理水平得到提高，引入了内部控制和风险管理机制，采用了利润最大化战略。主要的证券公司被重组，建立了证券公司处置和投资者保护机制。保险部门改革也取得进展。

2. 各项金融改革政策尚在推进，但扭曲仍然存在。这些扭曲与现行的利率政策、信贷数量指导、有限的投资渠道和因政府隐性担保而产生的道德风险等因素有关。因此，中国金融体系呈现如下特征：（1）资金成本过低，没有向国内居民支付足够报酬；（2）价格倾向于偏离市场出清状态；（3）在对大型国有企业债务隐性担保的情况下，缺乏足够动力对风险进行定价；[①]（4）重视减少银行资产负债表中的不良贷款；（5）结构流动性较高；（6）存在将信贷转向表外的动力；（7）金融体系中的非国有股权（包括外资股权）仍然有限。直接配置和信贷定价有力地支持了中国经济的强劲增长，这是因为具有高增长潜力的部门比较容易识别，但这也导致了产能过剩、潜在的资产泡沫和需要运用公共资金对银行进行注资等问题。

3. 信贷主要通过银行体系发放，国内资本市场的作用有限（图1）。2009年底，中国商业银行贷款占金融体系总资产的比率大于其他国家。非银行金融机构（包括信托投资公司、金融租赁公司、财务公司）一直在发展（附表4）。

4. 金融部门发展状况从储蓄存款占比之高中可见一斑，这是因为替代性投资渠道有限（图2）。存款占银行体系负债的比率超过80％，且以平均每年19％的速度增长。近年来，由于企业较强的盈利能力，以及居民存款因风险偏好的增加和较低

---

① 信贷利率上限已取消，但银行不会上浮信贷利率，这反映了银行存在贷款给安全借款人（有政府隐性担保）的动力，以及风险定价能力不足的问题。

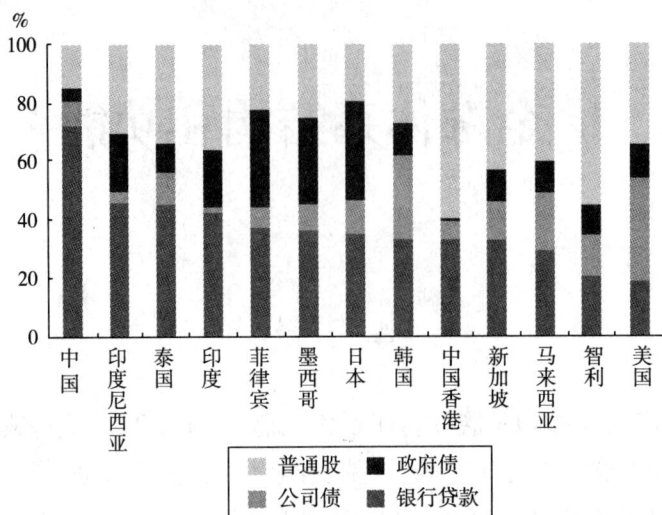

数据来源：毕马威。

图1　2009年部分国家（地区）金融体系规模

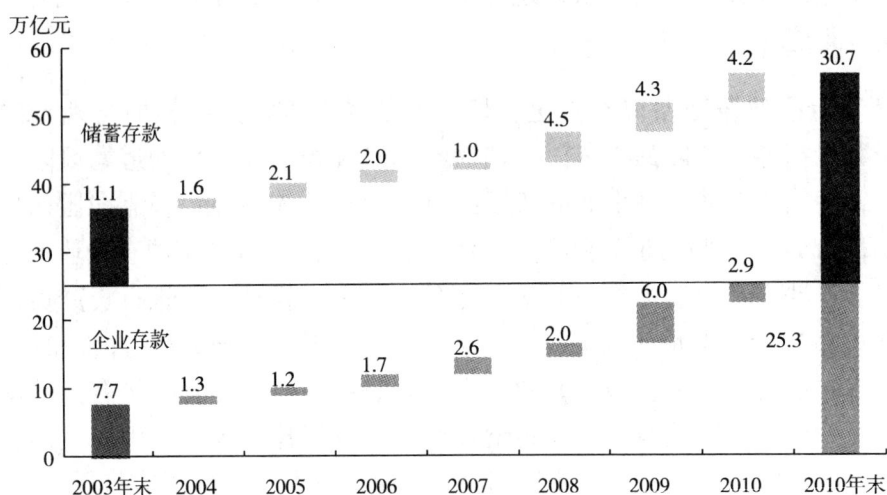

数据来源：中国银监会，国际货币基金组织人员计算。

图2　中国银行体系存款余额及增量

的存款利率而转移，企业存款成为银行资金增长的主要驱动力。

B. 宏观金融环境

5. **在过去的三十年里，在高投资和信贷高速增长的支持下，中国经济保持了非常高的增速（附表3）。** 自1978年改革开放以来，中国经济以年均两位数的速度增长，同时通胀率保持相对低位，反映了生产率的快速提高及源于高投资水平的产能增加。虽然存在或有负债，但公共债务水平仍然相对较低。由于结构流动性较高、利率较低、替代投资工具缺乏，中国经济有出现资产泡沫的可能，尤其是在股票市场和房地产市场。

6. 在宏观经济政策转型过程中，金融体系具有直接的、非常重要的作用。 中国的宏观金融关联性体现在五个方面：（1）银行体系通过信贷渠道为准财政政策直接提供便利。（2）银行体系为货币政策直接提供便利，但信贷增长目标降低了信贷配置的效率。（3）资本的低成本扭曲了经济中储蓄与投资的平衡。（4）欠发达的资本市场使公司融资和居民投资的替代选择非常有限，不利于解决金融体系中的结构性问题，如：低储蓄回报率；高预防性储蓄（通过银行）；由于不能从资本市场获得资金，私营企业的储蓄率过高；金融体系继续以银行为主导；潜在的资产泡沫。（5）市场缺乏竞争，或大型企业的所有制抑制了竞争。

C. 金融监管框架

7. 金融监管明显改善，但监管效率、质量及响应速度仍需进一步提高。 FSAP评估表明，中国遵守国际标准的程度很高。但从长期看，必须在监管控制和允许金融体系进行有益的创新和发展这两者之间进行适当平衡。此次评估给出的改进建议是：（1）加强监管机构的操作独立性；（2）提升技能；（3）提升风险监测能力；（4）增加资源；（5）加强部门间的协调。

8. 银行监管

a. 银监会在改进银行监管框架方面取得长足进展。 银监会虽然有明确的维护银行体系安全和稳健的职责，但由于国家主导的银行体系不断地被用来支持经济发展和信贷扩张，银监会的操作独立性受到影响。长期来看，确保银监会的操作独立性，使其能够充分履行自己的职责显得尤为重要。这应当包括充足的预算和监管资源，使其能够适应中国银行业日益增长的规模和复杂性。

b. 银行业法律法规框架逐步与国际标准接轨，但仍存在差距。 这些差距包括：（1）缺乏对间接控制权变更、银行受益权人认定和客户识别的具体规定；（2）有效识别关联方的规定不够充分；（3）缺乏银行处置的法律框架。

9. 证券公司和证券市场监管

a. 证监会推进监管改革以支持金融体系的市场化发展。 尽管已建立一套可靠的检查和监督机制，但需要进一步强化对非法投资行为的查处以及对对冲基金和私募股权基金的监测。虽然投入了大量资源监测并打击内幕交易和市场操纵，但仍需加大投入。证监会应对交易所引入正式的现场检查机制，加大监管力度。进一步加强对基于风险管理的净资本规则和"了解你的客户"规则的执行和监测。

b. 需进一步完善证券市场法律框架，以适应市场发展的需要。 需要改进的方面包括：商业法庭、针对非法投资活动的查处以及对不公平交易活动的监测与打击。证监会需要更大的操作独立性，从而更有效地履行其法定职责而不受到干涉。考虑到市场的快速发展以及市场约束的作用尚不明显，证监会的预算应更具灵活性。会计和审计人员的专业素质取得了很大进步，但随着市场规模的扩大和复杂程度的提高，仍需在人员规模和专业能力方面继续改进。

10. 保险监管

a. 保监会建立了以公司治理、消费者保护和风险管理为重点的综合监管框架，但需在以下方面加以完善：（1）恢复使用早期预警比率，加强非现场监测；（2）加强非寿险负债和偿付能力监管；（3）在拓展投资渠道的同时，对寿险加强基于风险管理的偿付准备金最低要求；（4）出台明晰的法规，以利于保险公司通过托管或业务转移的方式退出市场；（5）加强人民银行与保监会在反洗钱领域的合作和信息共享。此外，应采取严格措施限制偿付能力低于100%的保险公司开展新业务。

b. 保监会的职责和操作独立性需要加强。 应重新审视保监会的行业发展职能，使其专注于自己的真正职能。保监会的预算应当保证其有充足的组织和行业资源。目前来看，随着市场和基于风险管理的监管机制的逐步成熟，应重新考量基于规则的监管体系。

11. 对其他金融机构的监管

a. 对其他金融机构进行监管，旨在限制其与正规银行部门间的关联性。 除商业银行和政策性银行外，信贷体系中还存在大量其他类型的非银行金融机构。信托公司、企业集团财务公司、租赁公司等机构由银监会负责监管。此外，还有一些由地方政府颁发牌照的非正规金融机构（如典当行、担保公司、小额贷款公司等）和偶尔由人民银行调查但未受监管的机构（非正规银行）。

b. 需要明确对影子银行的监管政策及监管职责。 目前，银监会与国家发展和改革委员会认为，影子银行体系主要由私募股权（其中大多数尚未受到监管）、非正规放贷者和存款吸收者（由人民银行和银监会监测）构成。应当明确对影子银行的监管政策和监管职责，以信息共享备忘录为基础，加强跨部门协调机制，防止系统性风险通过跨市场金融产品或业务而积聚。

II. 银行业

12. 银行体系由大型商业银行和股份制商业银行主导。 2010年底，5家大型商业银行和12家股份制商业银行的资产总和占商业银行总资产的83%（图3）。所有的大型商业银行和大多数股份制商业银行的所有权或部分所有权归属于政府，因此基本由政府控制。深化银行业的商业化转型将有助于推进整个金融业的商业化发展。

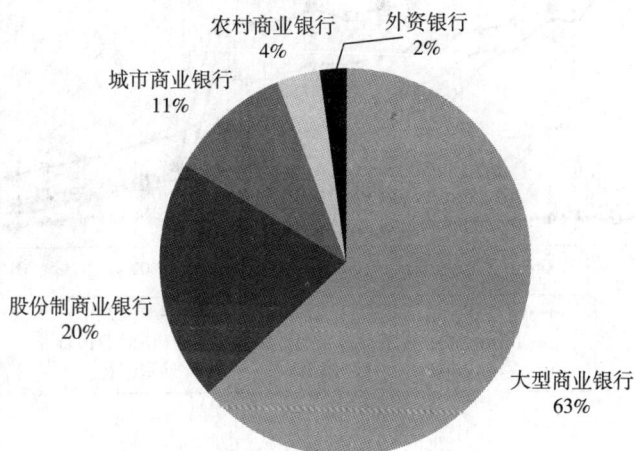

数据来源：中国银监会；国际货币基金组织人员计算。

图3　中国银行体系规模（截至2010年底）

13. 宏观经济刺激政策等因素导致银行业资产负债规模快速扩张。 基础设施建设和交通运输业的信贷需求因此而增加，其中大部分信贷需求来自于地方政府融资平台。2009年的经济刺激政策导致地方政府融资平台快速增长。由于地方财政收入和支出不匹配，且地方政府无法直接融资，这就使得在快速发展经济和避免过度金融风险之间很难取得平衡。

14. 信贷和资产负债表快速扩张给银行业带来了高利润，这也与宏观经济刺激政策有关。 大部分信贷需求来自于地方政府，再加上购买房产的信贷需求、大额外资流入引起的信用创造等，导致了人民币贷款的快速扩张。此外，自2009年第二季度以来，由于银行大力推广理财产品，其表外风险敞口迅速增加。

15. 银行的不良贷款率呈下降趋势，到2010年底降至1.1%（图4）。 不良贷款

11

率的下降是由于信贷的高速扩张和不良贷款余额的大幅下降所致。不良贷款余额从2005年底的1.3万亿元下降至2010年底的4 340亿元，主要原因是2008年对某大型银行8 160亿元不良贷款的剥离和处置。此外，一些不良贷款转为正常类、银行风险管理水平提高等因素，也有利于防止不良贷款水平的上升。

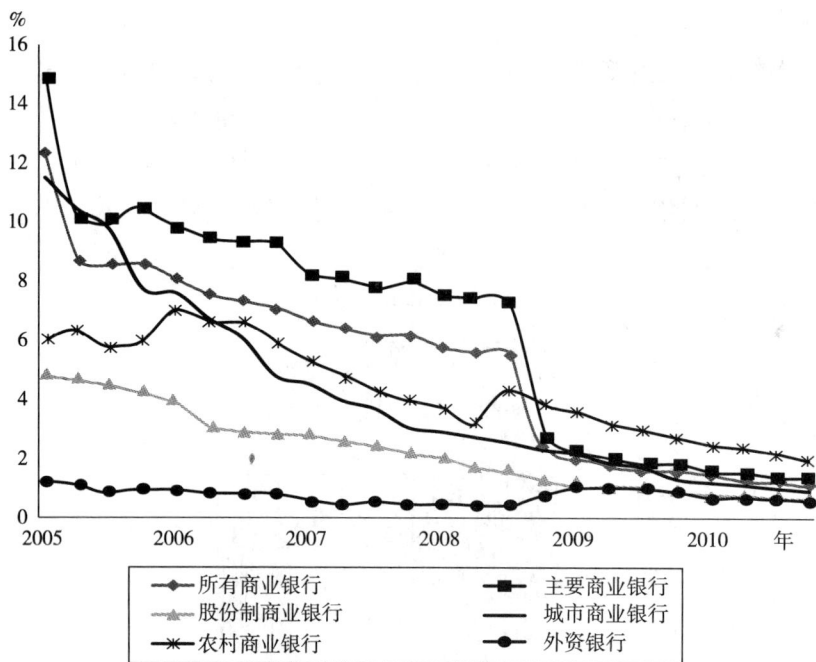

数据来源：CEIC数据库。

图4 中国不良贷款率

16. 银行资金来源保持稳定，但长期贷款的增加使银行面临期限错配的挑战。大量低成本存款有助于银行资金来源的稳定。2008年以来，企业存款的不断增加已成为存款增加的主要动力。期限错配问题在上升。银行资产的期限因项目投资日益依赖中长期贷款而拉长。由于贷款可定期重新定价，因此，利率错配风险有限，但期限错配给银行流动性管理带来了挑战。

17. 压力测试覆盖了5家大型银行和12家股份制商业银行，由FSAP评估团和当局共同开展。与其他银行相比，这17家银行有更全面的信息披露和更成熟的风险管理体系。压力测试由FSAP评估团与人民银行、银监会密切合作完成。压力测试包括一系列单因素冲击和宏观经济情景分析，但受到数据缺乏的限制。冲击强度的设定考虑到了中国和其他国家的历史经验，以及过去的FSAP实践。单因素敏感性分析的结果表明，银行体系能够承受一系列因素的单独冲击。宏观情景分析的结果表明，如果几个主要冲击同时发生，银行体系将会受到严重影响。

Ⅲ. 促进债券市场和股票市场发展

18. 作为银行贷款的替代性融资渠道，资本市场在过去五年间得到了发展（附表6），但仍有巨大的增长潜力有待挖掘。近年来，尽管在建立多层次资本市场方面取得了一些进展，一定程度上满足了高信用级别的大型国有企业和中小企业的融资需求。但是，资本市场在满足低信用级别（即使高于投资级别）的大企业和中小企业融资需求方面仍有很大的改进空间。由于银行在金融部门占主要地位，因此要使资本市场发展成为有效的融资渠道还面临诸多挑战。

19. 虽然银行脱媒的趋势不断深化，但银行部门仍有望继续在资本市场发展中扮演重要角色。作为发行人、承销商、分销商、投资者和流动性提供者，银行部门将对固定收益市场的发展速度和质量产生显著影响。该市场的发展速度还取决于政府的利率改革进程。

20. 完善的政府债券市场对于建立更加多元化和专业化的固定收益市场至关重要。目前的无风险收益率曲线并不均衡，因为在曲线短端，国债与中央银行票据交织，而在中端，又与流动性更强的政策性银行债券并存（图5）。中央银行票据的频繁使用对构建市场基础、促进债券市场成熟发展起到了重要作用。但长期来看，中央银行票据的持续大量发行，可能需要人民银行与财政部在期限相似的工具发行政

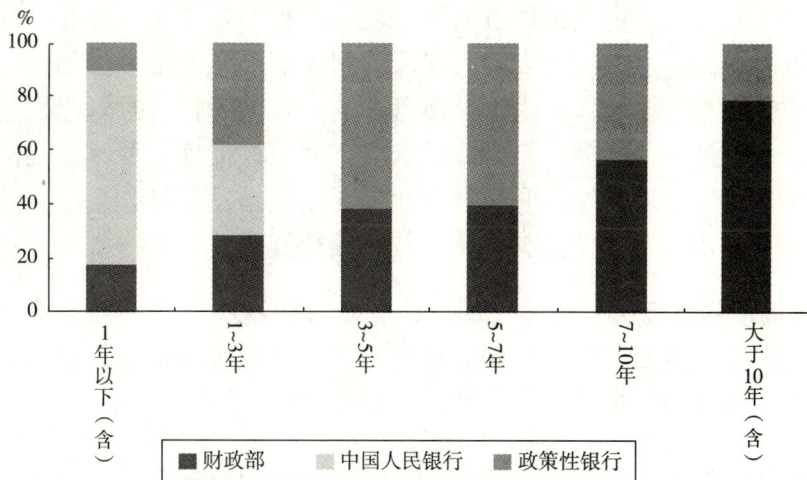

数据来源：中国债券信息网。

图5　中国各公共部门债券的期限分布

策方面进一步协调。这是成熟的新兴市场经济体为构建无风险收益率曲线所采取的普遍做法，这些经济体往往面临大量资本流入，需要进行大量的流动性对冲操作。可以预见的是，随着中国经济的持续发展和资本流入量的下降，这种不均衡将随着对冲需求的降低而得到缓解。

21. **需要采取更加积极、可持续的措施来构建利率基准。**包括进一步加强财政部和人民银行在相同期限债务工具和债务管理方面的协作，以促进市场基准的构建。这有助于为市场参与者提供清晰的收益率曲线，在促进债券市场发展的同时，支持二级市场流动性和利率对冲工具的发展。

22. **中国目前的固定收益市场监管涉及三个机构（人民银行、发展改革委和证监会）。**三者间的职责划分有待进一步明晰，以保持监管规则的一致性。即使监管者不同，对于相似类型的市场参与者应适用于同样的监管规则。一个可能的选择是，尊重现有的市场实践，在批发市场和零售市场间划分监管职责，并加强监管的一致性，增强市场间的连通性（如银行间市场与交易所固定收益市场之间的连通性）。此外，也可借鉴其他方式达到此目的。

23. **在促进地方政府债券市场发展的过程中，需仔细考量伴生风险并保证及时披露信息和数据。**这是保证这些风险既不会转化为政府的或有负债，也不会对中国固定收益市场产生负面影响的关键所在。省级政府需要有足够的技术力量来发行和管理债务，并对债务可持续性定期进行分析。至关重要的一点是要确保投资者的多样化，同时商业银行不是被动地投资于地方政府债券。

24. **应继续发展固定收益市场，以满足信用级别低但可靠企业的融资需求。**这将使中小企业和其他私营企业得以进入该市场。过去的一年里，已有一些中小企业融资方面的创新，促进了市场的发展。在低信用级别公司的准入方面，当局对相关风险管理的担忧是有道理的，一个更灵活可行的方式是为符合投资级别的公司设立一个子市场。为达到这一目标，需要从供求两方面采取措施，使得适当的机构投资者能够投资于这些工具。此外，取消对企业市场化债券发行累计余额不超过其净资产40%的限制，将有助于扩大直接融资以代替银行贷款。

25. **银行间债券市场仍有改善空间。**改进做市商制度对价格的形成和无风险收益率曲线的完善至关重要，财政部和人民银行已经开始考虑此事。此外，通过为非银行类市场参与者提供更多的机会，可进一步改善市场流动性。

26. **回购市场发展迅速，但由于法律和操作方面的限制，其经济影响有限。**质押式回购在回购市场中占主导地位，买断式回购的使用有限，且担保品不能重复质押，这不仅限制了市场流动性，而且还限制了货币市场与政府债券市场之间的必要联系。在中国这样的大市场中，正规的买断式回购规模非常小，从而导致了非正规回购市场的出现。因此，使买断式回购交易规范化、标准化，对于保持固定收益市场的效率和完整性至关重要。

27. 有效对冲工具（如利率衍生品）的不发达也阻碍了资本市场的进一步发展。国债的低流动性限制了其发展。完善国债发行政策、二级市场组织及回购政策，将为衍生品市场建设提供健全的框架。

28. 中国股票市场已取得长足发展，但仍面临诸多挑战。挑战之一是将上海证券交易所建设成为大企业融资而非主要为国有企业融资的场所。近年来，在技术和监管方面已采取措施，但要提高上市公司和国有企业流通股比率仍面临挑战。另一个挑战是更好地满足中小企业的融资需求。作为建设多层次资本市场的举措，深圳证券交易所推出了主板、中小板（2004年）和创业板（2009年），这一方向是正确的，将会为更多的企业提供有效的融资渠道。

29. 对不同类型的机构投资者（共同基金、养老基金、保险公司）的监管政策应统一，以发展多元化的机构投资者基础，这对于中国资本市场的发展至关重要。机构投资者的不断发展壮大，有利于增加资本配置的效率、支撑证券市场扩容（包括上市公司数量和已上市股本比例）并降低市场波动性。对于固定收益市场，在审慎原则下进一步增强投资的灵活性，将有利于大量具有投资级别的私营公司进入这个市场。

30. 发展稳健的投资者基础富有挑战，需要采取以下措施：一是在发展机构投资者过程中，要努力创造条件发挥银行作为资产管理公司所有者或分销商的重要作用；二是在制定集合投资计划的监管规则时，要与资本市场向私营企业扩大开放的趋势保持一致；三是在理财公司快速发展过程中，监测可能出现的监管套利机会。

Ⅳ. 发展稳健的保险业

31. 中国保险业发展迅速，但仍有进一步发展的空间。截至 2009 年底，保险业管理的资产不足国内个人银行存款的 11%。中国保险业保费收入已在世界排名第六，反映了中国巨大的人口规模和相对较大的寿险业（个人产品）市场规模。但仍有进一步发展的空间。尤其是，考虑到现有的收入水平和结构，非寿险业（财产保险和意外险）的保险深度比预期的要低。

32. 快速增长伴随着重要风险。保险公司的实际保费收入年均增长率超过 15%，近期这一态势还将持续。但与此同时，非寿险业的资本利润率不够高，不能使资本维持在足以应对基本风险因素增加的水平。

33. 按现行的会计方法，近十年来获得保险经营牌照的 87 家保险公司中，大部分持续亏损。这些公司的经济价值（基于未来现金流）实际上在增加，其亏损多数来自开办费用和业务快速扩张。但是，有些保险公司的偿付能力已经低于或接近 100%，保监会需要密切监测这些公司的业务模式是否有缺陷。快速扩张（典型的方法是通过有竞争力的佣金和保险产品定价）也给大型保险公司造成盈利压力。虽然绝大多数保险公司能够满足目前的最低偿付能力要求，但总体偿付能力需要加强。目前的偿付比率分布状况严重增加了监管负担，也会给保险公司发展带来不利影响。

34. 在稳定非寿险业技术准备金方面，保监会最近采取的措施似乎是有效的。在资本要求方面采取的措施主要包括：允许大型保险公司（多数是国家或省级政府控制的保险公司）通过上市筹资，允许高比例的再保险，允许保险公司经核准后发行次级债以满足偿付能力要求，对某些情况采取一定宽容度。保监会已经在研究审查偿付能力标准问题。加快实施更审慎的监管标准是可取的，对于寿险部门来说，随着投资渠道的拓宽，情况尤其如此。

35. 通过引进更全面的以风险管理为基础的资本要求并要求股东适时执行，来构建合理的策略。应加强对非寿险理赔准备金计提的精算监管，并明确自愿结束业务并退出市场的规则和程序。还可以采取其他有效措施使保险公司能获得更高、更稳定的资本利润率。包括：将机动车交通事故责任强制保险纳入互助共保池，由经批准的保险公司进行管理；引进能够有效反映风险的定价机制，并类似地开发经适当定价的（可能享受补贴的）巨灾险共保池。

36. 应采取更审慎的措施，如要求寿险公司指定与算术准备金和最低资本要求相匹配的资产，并且不能用做借款的抵押品（尽管允许保险公司开展回购可以增加收益，只要保险公司保留相关资产的所有权）。在公司解散时，职工的工资和奖金及担保债权的清偿优先于寿险保单持有人的做法与国际最佳实践相反。

37. 应重新评估有关审慎治理的规则。目前允许进行关联交易并就此制定了一些治理规则，但这并不能完全有效防止不正当行为的发生。随着保险集团和金融控股公司增多，超过一定规模的关联交易及对管理层和职工发放的贷款，应获得保监会的批准，并在年度报表中予以披露。

V. 养老金行业面临的挑战

38. 中国已逐步建立起多支柱的养老金体系，但仍面临相当大的挑战。 第一支柱即基本养老保险体系包括非积累制和部分积累制两类。第二支柱即企业年金体系，是自愿性的企业补充养老金体制。第三支柱包括个人和企业养老金计划，比年金更灵活，但仍未发展起来。每一个支柱都面临挑战，需要当局认真应对。

39. 第一支柱的养老基金结余面临投资效率不高的问题。 第一支柱的养老基金体系包括两个层次：第一层次是传统的现收现付制；第二层次是部分积累制，即个人拥有账户，由政府负责投资管理。由于缺乏足够的资金支持向全积累制转化，许多地方政府利用第二层次的个人账户资金来弥补第一层次中的资金缺口。部分地方政府正在做实个人账户，但大部分养老金资产投资于低收益的银行存款和短期国债。目前，有九个省的第二养老金支柱中的部分资产（中央政府对个人账户的补贴）由全国社保基金理事会负责投资运营，这将成为全国普遍采用的模式。

40. 改进养老金投资策略对促进资本市场发展至关重要。 保本型投资策略作为养老金制度的普遍投资策略，不能产生足够的回报满足未来的养老金需求。长远看，投资策略应偏重于股权和长期债券。投资监管应摈弃短期业绩评价，而应重点关注投资策略与长期目标的匹配。

41. 企业年金覆盖了国有企业的大部分职工。 有限的税收优惠、复杂的企业年金治理框架以及不完善的监管框架等因素阻碍了企业年金的发展。由于企业年金监管框架与中小企业劳动合同管理框架有冲突，且劳动合同的执行力度也不够，因此企业年金的增速不可能与城市就业增速相匹配。

42. 鉴于中国的储蓄文化传统，可考虑发展个人养老金计划。 例如，通过个人所得税的激励[②]或政府提供配套资金支持（针对低收入者），使得部分预防性储蓄资金进入个人养老储蓄账户。这将惠及一大批目前仍未获得正式养老储蓄计划的人群。个人养老金计划可为参与者提供与其长期目标相一致的标准化养老金产品。尽管不同的机构获准提供的产品不同，但这些个人养老金计划的投资策略应与独立的专业机构或专家根据生命周期设计的基准投资组合相匹配。

---

② 当前的个人所得税将收入按其来源进行区分，而不是将全部收入视为一个整体，这使得此类激励的设计更富有挑战性。应当注意确保使目标群体成为最能受益的群体。鉴于部分人没有被纳入正式的养老金体系，或许激励措施应仅针对此类群体。

VI. 促进普惠金融的政策和战略

43. 中国在一些以广泛网络和技术改进为基础的金融服务领域发展迅速，但对于农村和城市居民以及小微企业而言，金融服务的可获得性仍然有限。农村居民对信贷的需求在一定程度上由非正规金融满足。替代性金融服务，如非寿险、保理和租赁，仍处于初级阶段。

44. **中国在推进普惠金融发展方面潜力巨大。** 为挖掘这一潜力，需要考虑以下几方面：（1）进一步深化金融机构改革，发掘其为有效益的客户提供金融服务和产品的潜力；（2）改革政府在金融服务提供中的角色和职能；（3）进一步完善金融基础设施和金融监管。

45. **应制定综合、统一的农村和小微企业融资战略，并使之不断完善。** 由于城镇化、工业化以及人口流动的快速发展，农村和微型金融的商业可持续性发生了改变，对政策导向型金融服务的需求有所减少。应制定政策，提高以商业原则为基础的、便捷且可持续的金融服务和产品的可获得性。政府的主要作用是提供合适的环境和金融基础设施，使那些治理结构良好并接受监管的金融机构在为农村和小微企业提供服务方面展开竞争。需要明确政府的角色和职能，并进一步采取措施改进普惠金融领域的监管有效性[3]。农村和小微企业金融当前还存在一些限制和障碍（如在市场准入、融资、区域扩张以及移动银行业务等方面），应认真考虑。

46. **应进一步发掘金融机构在拓宽金融可获得性方面的潜力。** 许多银行已开始探索针对农村居民和小微企业的商业化信贷之路。新型农村金融机构（如村镇银行、贷款公司和农村资金互助合作社）和小额贷款公司带来了一些竞争压力，但其作用的发挥还需假以时日。为进一步扩大成果，需要深化对国有金融机构——特别是农业发展银行和邮政储蓄银行——以及农村信用合作社的改革，使其进一步完善公司治理和风险管理。

47. **为建立普惠金融框架，当局应当考虑在法律等方面进行改革。** 重点是：（1）扩大征信系统的覆盖范围；（2）全国性的担保交易框架及庭外和解；（3）促进保理和租赁行业发展，作为小微企业融资的替代方式；（4）为非正规贷款者的存在和业务运作制定规则；（5）对政策性贷款项目进行仔细的绩效评估；（6）设计统计系

---

③ 众所周知，有许多类型的金融机构在地方注册，却很少受到监管甚至不受监管。

统，强调服务覆盖的实际范围（以小额贷款和客户的数量来衡量）、效率和金融可持续性。

48. 进一步放松贷款利率管制，对促进农村和小微企业信贷商业化、可持续发展至关重要。金融机构在面向低端市场时会面临高成本。贷款利率上限限制将导致不公平竞争，可能阻碍农村信用社向那些符合贷款条件的微型和小型借款人提供服务。最高人民法院关于高利贷的规定不利于正规部门给这一群体发放贷款，使其不得不从黑市上以更高的利率进行融资。有必要解决上述矛盾以提高金融可获得性。

49. 政府应改进对金融可获得性的度量，实施切实可行的监测和评价措施，并指导公共政策的制定。使用县域金融机构信贷作为涉农贷款的统计标准具有误导性。同样，中国的中小企业定义包含了一些规模较大的企业，而不仅仅是小型客户。应当考虑设计与国际实践相一致的统计系统，注重服务覆盖的实际范围（以小额贷款和客户的数量来衡量）、效率和金融可持续性。

VII. 金融市场和市场基础设施

A. 金融稳定和危机管理

50. 需要审视监管结构，确保其能够应对金融部门迅速发展带来的挑战。 中国金融监管采取按机构监管的方式，三个独立的委员会与人民银行共同承担责任（附表7）。国务院对金融体系负总责。2008 年6 月，国务院设立并主持了一个出主要金融管理部门参与的高级别委员会来履行这一职责。评估团建议，应根据这一特别委员会的经验，建立一个常设的金融稳定委员会。

51. 中国的危机管理安排属于国务院的职权范围。 迄今，国务院在处理金融问题时更倾向于采用"不关闭"的处置方式。这可能由政府作为危机管理者和机构所有者的双重角色所决定。结果，政府自1999 年开始向资本不足的银行注入资本，并从银行向资产管理公司④剥离不良资产，以维护银行资产负债表的稳健。

52. 应考虑建立相应制度安排并增加处置工具，从而使对问题银行实施"关闭处置"成为可行的政策选择。 处置工具包括：赋予监管者对濒临倒闭金融机构及时干预的法律权力；赋予一个独立部门用于关闭、注资或者出售这类机构的资源和管理被干预机构及其资产的权力。中国当局对引入存款保险制度已考虑很久，鉴于中国金融体系中存在大量存款类机构以及降低风险敞口的需要，应该加快推进这项工作。

B. 货币市场、外汇市场和银行间市场

53. 利率管制和汇率制度抑制了金融发展和创新。 继续推进利率市场化和人民币汇率制度改革将有助于金融发展和创新。批发性利率和衍生品价格未受管制。尽管2005 年以来在增强汇率灵活性方面取得了一定进展，但银行间市场人民币兑美元现货市场汇率日内波动幅度被限制在 ±0.5%，汇率中间价的日间波动实际上也未超过这个幅度，同时零售利率仍然受到管制。这就限制了金融机构和公司企业的汇率

---

④ 资产管理公司的建立是为了帮助银行重组，应制定资产管理公司发展战略。建议将资产管理公司转型为商业实体，以减少道德风险，鼓励银行进行高质量的风险分析。与此同时，应要求资产管理公司定期公布财务报表和经营报告。

风险敞口和利率风险敞口，从而降低了对套期保值产品的需求以及金融市场和产品创新的动力。人民银行目前正在积极研究和引导金融机构创新汇率避险工具。

54. 改进政府债券发行策略、继续推进利率市场化改革并解决其他价格扭曲问题，将能够提高债券市场的效率。 发行策略可以作为提高二级市场流动性的一种工具。套利机会在收益率曲线的不同部分依然存在。

C. 系统流动性

55. 充足的流动性降低了近期内发生系统流动性危机的风险，但使得整体流动性管理更加复杂化。 更多地使用间接工具可改善人民银行的整体流动性管理。随着资本管制面临更多挑战、金融市场进一步发展、中国日益融入国际金融体系，人民银行对于基础货币的控制日趋困难。这就要求更多地使用间接工具。初期，人民银行可以一种短期货币市场利率为目标进行试点。

56. 降低存款准备金要求，并引入日均存款准备金机制，有助于金融机构进行流动性管理，进一步稳定流动性。 应考虑对金融机构进行日均准备金试点，包括具有结构性资金盈余的机构和持续性资金短缺的机构。为控制人民银行流动性管理操作对财政部发行收益的影响，这两个部门之间应就发行相同期限产品加强合作。通过分析不同的模式（如墨西哥、巴西的模式）来建立适合于中国的框架。面临的挑战是既要保持人民银行的自主性以引导短期利率，使与其货币政策目标相符，必要时开展冲销操作，同时也要有利于财政部不断完善无风险收益率曲线。此外，金融机构对人民银行存贷款便利的获得应更加自主和透明，并通过定价机制来解决道德风险问题。

D. 支付和证券结算系统

57. 人民银行对中国支付清算体系（CNPS）进行了全面改革。 大额支付系统（HVPS）是中国支付清算体系的核心，属于系统重要性支付系统。针对大额支付系统的评估表明，该系统大致遵守《系统重要性支付系统核心原则》，但仍有改进的空间，尤其是在法律框架和监管制度安排方面。当局应确保支付、衍生品和证券结算的最终性得到法律的完全保护。在监管方面，人民银行应明确支付系统监管政策，确定履职范围、主要政策和工具。建议人民银行对中国外汇交易中心（CFETS）进行更为积极的监管。

58. FSAP 评估团针对证券和衍生品结算系统开展的评估表明该系统大致符合国际标准， 但在以下方面仍有待改进：

- 对于进行债券市场结算的中央国债登记结算有限责任公司的系统：法律基础、预结算和结算风险、公司治理、透明度和监管。

- 对于进行交易所证券交易结算的中国证券登记结算有限责任公司的系统：应确保进一步加强中央对手方的稳健性和增加透明度。

- 对于开展商品期货市场交易结算的上海期货交易所（SHFE）的系统：法律基础、保证金要求和透明度。

E. 法律法规结构

59. **金融部门法律框架结构的发展较为分散。**应定期评估这一框架，以有效识别和修订相关规则。尽管当局做了大量的工作以确保规则制定的有效性，包括公开披露、大范围征求意见，以及全国人大常委会和国务院为适时改革而进行的干预等，但仍有很多工作要做，以确保通过建立反馈机制使法律得到有效实施。因此，有必要全面清理金融业法律中存在的空白、重复和表述不清之处。

60. **在制定和执行法律过程中，应更多地采取基于原则的监管方式，这将是有益的。**目前的监管方式以规则为基础，金融机构在规则应用方面缺乏灵活性，盲目地相信金融机构完全符合规则，其结果是合规成本非常高。基于规则的监管方式也许是合适的，但从长远看，应考虑采取更基于原则的方式。

61. **应重新审视破产程序和债权人保护的法律框架，以提供有效的退出机制。**在部分行业，尚未制定关于金融机构破产的详细法律。关于破产的法律框架有待改进，包括开展阈值法压力测试、未来索赔应对以及跨境破产处置的详细法规。此外，应加强消费者保护，包括加强法庭执行合同的能力、发挥消费者组织的积极作用、通过制定市场行为准则来强化法律对个人数据和隐私的保护。

F. 会计和审计[5]

62. **中国的商业银行已经采用了新版《中国会计准则》（CAS），该准则已与《国际财务报告准则》（IFRS）基本趋同。**2007年，财政部首次要求执行新版会计准则，包括一项基本准则和38项企业会计准则。审计从业者的能力存在差异，需予以关注，确保小型金融机构的财务报表质量能与大型机构的相匹配。需要加强对审计师独立性和专业性的监管。

---

[5] 世界银行：*Report on the Observance of Standards and Codes-Accounting and Auditing*，2009 。

G. 市场诚信

63. 中国在构建反洗钱和反恐融资体系方面取得重大进展。2007 年反洗钱金融行动特别工作组（FATF）互评估报告显示，中国反洗钱和反恐融资体系较好，但部分领域尚有待改进。之后，反洗钱和反恐融资法律体系不断完善。中国已经向 FATF 提交了一系列后续报告，陈述其在薄弱环节的改进情况。基于此，FATF 全会认为，目前中国反洗钱体系大致符合 FATF 的标准。但是，仍然存在两处不足：（1）根据中国的法律和司法实践，当局或金融机构难以识别法人机构受益权人的身份。（2）预防措施未充分延伸至非金融业务和从业人员。

附表1 主要建议

建 议	优先度	时间框架
推进商业化		
1. 继续推进利率和汇率改革进程，同时确保金融机构能够进行适当的信用风险管理。	高	中期
2. 明确区分政策性金融机构和商业性金融机构的作用和功能。	中	中期
3. 将四家资产管理公司转型为商业化实体，作为第一步，要求其定期公布财务报表和管理报告。	中	中期
提高机构和监管框架的效率		
4. 赋予人民银行和三个监管委员会以专责、操作自主权和灵活性、充实资金和熟练人员，并加强部门间合作，以应对快速发展的金融部门带来的挑战。	高	中期
5. 建立针对金融控股公司、金融集团和非正规金融企业的监管框架。过渡期内，任何受监管机构的并购活动都必须得到负责相应金融机构的监管委员会的批准。	中	近期
6. 在中国银监会的风险评级体系中推行更具前瞻性的信用风险评估，消除与信用风险和市场风险资本框架的偏差。	中	近期
7. 实施一个正式规划，使中国证监会据以定期对交易所进行全面的现场检查，以加强监督。	中	近期
8. 对保险公司实行风险资本偿付能力制度，并给予其适当的过渡期，限制偿付能力水平低于100%的保险公司开展新业务。	中	中期
9. 制定明确清晰的管理规定，为保险公司通过到期终止或资产转移而退出市场提供便利。	中	近期
10. 制定一部支付体系法，为支付、衍生产品和证券结算的最终性提供全面保护。	中	中期
11. 确保法人的受益所有权人和控制信息充分、准确，且主管部门能够随时获取。	高	中期
12. 改进人民银行和其他部门之间在反洗钱（AML）和其他监管问题方面的信息共享和协作安排。	高	中期
提升金融稳定、系统性风险监测、系统流动性和危机管理的框架		
13. 建立常设的金融稳定委员会，由人民银行作为其秘书处。	高	中期
14. 改进对金融机构数据的收集，包括其杠杆率、或有负债、表外头寸、未受监管产品以及跨境和部门风险敞口。	中	近期
15. 建立宏观审慎框架来衡量并管理系统性风险，这应该包括增加人民银行和监管机构的资源、提高其监测金融稳定和实施定期压力测试的能力。	高	近期

续表

建 议	优先度	时间框架
16. 通过市场化工具加强对结构流动性的对冲，并通过间接货币政策工具管理系统流动性的溢出效应。	高	近期
17. 实行平均准备金制度，以便利流动性管理并提高稳定性和效率。	高	近期
18. 开始试行短期回购利率目标制，作为间接流动性管理的尝试，并开始进行每日公开市场操作。	高	近期
19. 确保人民银行的存贷款便利操作的即时性和自动性，对所有国内注册机构实行统一的抵押品要求。	中	近期
20. 实行存款保险制度，为金融机构的有序关闭提供支持，并帮助理清或有负债。	中	近期
发展证券市场，将存款导向协议型和集合投资部门		
21. 确保监管规则的一致性，并明确监管责任，为固定收益市场的发展提供支持。	中	中期
22. 继续改进财政部和人民银行的债券发行策略，以帮助改进收益率曲线上各种期限产品的现有做市活动。	高	中期
23. 提升回购市场的管理和操作框架以提高市场流动性，加强风险管理，并强化货币和债券市场利率之间的联动。	中	近期
24. 放宽对公司市场化债券发行累计余额不能超过净资产40%的限制，以扩大其直接融资能力。	中	中期
25. 通过提升中央国债登记结算有限责任公司（CCDC）和中国证券登记结算有限责任公司（SD&C）之间的联系，加强银行间债券市场、上海证券交易所和深圳证券交易所之间的联动性，为这三个市场的进一步发展提供支持，并帮助其提高效率。	中	中期
26. 巩固多支柱养老保险体系，重点关注积累制基本养老保险。	中	中期
改善替代性融资渠道和可获得性		
27. 审视现有的政府规划，确定其在促进农村和小微企业融资方面是否有效，并制订综合且连贯的农村和小微企业融资战略。	高	中期
28. 进一步改革农村信用合作社，增强其作为金融产品和服务的商业提供者的效率和可持续性。	中	中期
29. 通过优化股权结构、公司化以及建立有效的公司治理，完成邮政储蓄银行的改革。	中	中期

注：①近期指3年内实施完毕；中期指3~5年内实施完毕。

②此表在《中国FSAP备忘录》基础上有所修改。

附表2　中国金融部门改革

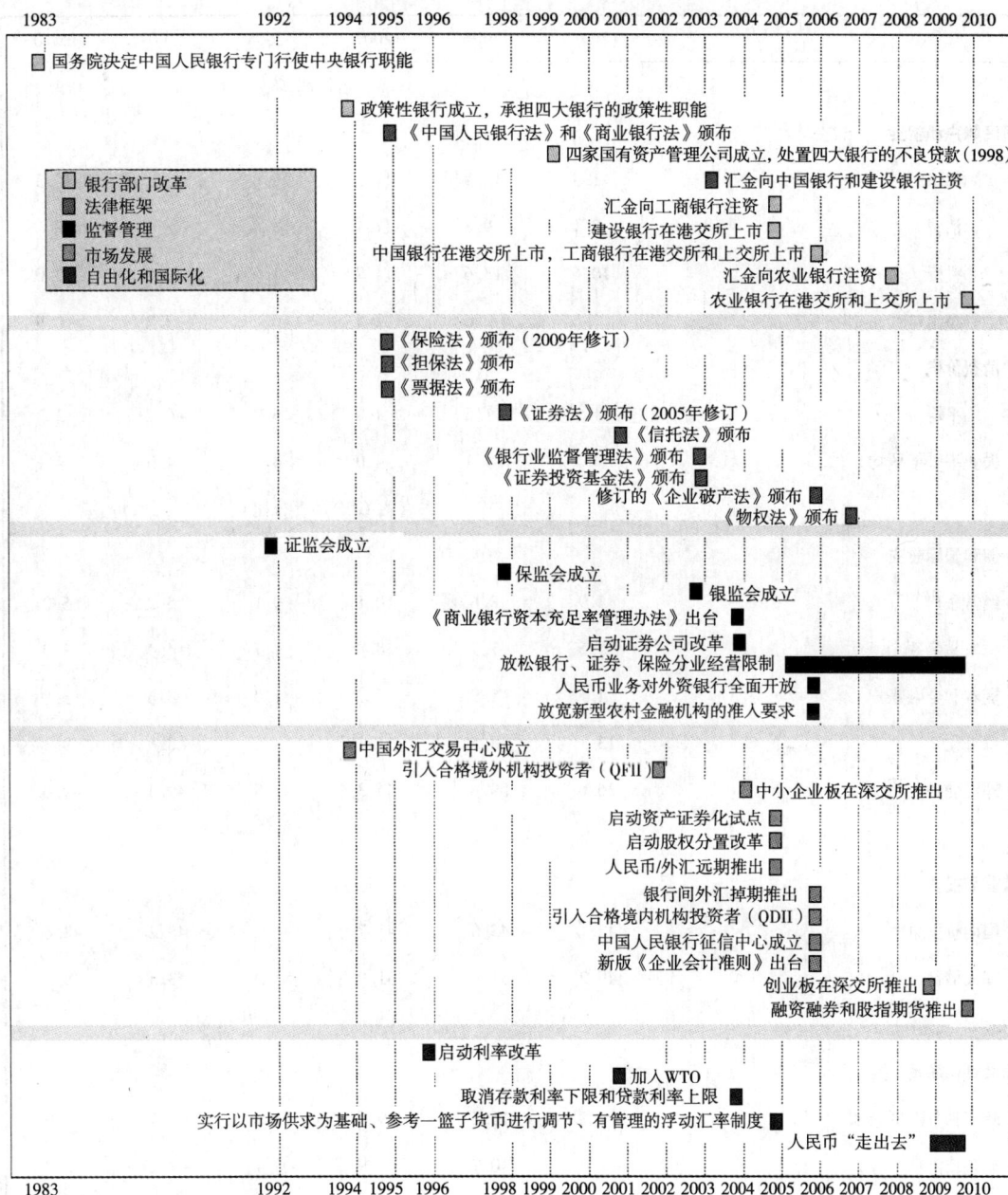

1983　　　　　　　　1992　　1994 1995 1996　　1998 1999 2000 2001 2002 2003 2004 2005 2006 2007 2008 2009 2010

■ 国务院决定中国人民银行专门行使中央银行职能

■ 政策性银行成立，承担四大银行的政策性职能
■ 《中国人民银行法》和《商业银行法》颁布
■ 四家国有资产管理公司成立，处置四大银行的不良贷款（1998）
■ 汇金向中国银行和建设银行注资
汇金向工商银行注资 ■
建设银行在港交所上市 ■
中国银行在港交所上市，工商银行在港交所和上交所上市 ■
汇金向农业银行注资 ■
农业银行在港交所和上交所上市 ■

□ 银行部门改革
■ 法律框架
■ 监督管理
□ 市场发展
■ 自由化和国际化

■ 《保险法》颁布（2009年修订）
■ 《担保法》颁布
■ 《票据法》颁布
■ 《证券法》颁布（2005年修订）
■ 《信托法》颁布
《银行业监督管理法》颁布 ■
《证券投资基金法》颁布 ■
修订的《企业破产法》颁布 ■
《物权法》颁布 ■

■ 证监会成立
■ 保监会成立
银监会成立 ■
《商业银行资本充足率管理办法》出台 ■
启动证券公司改革 ■
放松银行、证券、保险分业经营限制 ████████
人民币业务对外资银行全面开放 ■
放宽新型农村金融机构的准入要求 ■

■ 中国外汇交易中心成立
引入合格境外机构投资者（QFII）■
中小企业板在深交所推出 ■
启动资产证券化试点 ■
启动股权分置改革 ■
人民币/外汇远期推出 ■
银行间外汇掉期推出 ■
引入合格境内机构投资者（QDII）■
中国人民银行征信中心成立 ■
新版《企业会计准则》出台 ■
创业板在深交所推出 ■
融资融券和股指期货推出 ■

■ 启动利率改革
■ 加入WTO
取消存款利率下限和贷款利率上限 ■
实行以市场供求为基础、参考一篮子货币进行调节、有管理的浮动汇率制度
人民币"走出去" ████

1983　　　　　　　　1992　　1994 1995 1996　　1998 1999 2000 2001 2002 2003 2004 2005 2006 2007 2008 2009 2010

注：四大银行指工商银行、农业银行、中国银行和建设银行。这四家银行于近年进行了商业化改造。四大银行和交通银行一起统称为大型商业银行。

附表3 中国部分经济指标

	2005	2006	2007	2008	2009	2010
			(年增长率,%)			
国民账户和就业						
实际 GDP	11.3	12.7	14.2	9.6	9.2	10.3
消费	8.1	9.8	11.1	8.6	8.4	8.1
投资	10.6	13.6	14.7	11.0	20.8	12.0
净出口①	2.6	2.0	2.5	0.8	-3.7	0.9
消费价格						
平均	1.8	1.5	4.8	5.9	-0.7	3.3
失业率 (年平均)	4.2	4.1	4.0	4.2	4.3	4.1
			(占 GDP 的百分比)			
外债和国际收支						
经常账户	5.9	8.6	10.1	9.1	5.2	5.2
贸易余额	5.5	7.7	8.8	7.7	4.4	3.9
资本和金融账户	4.5	1.9	2.7	1.0	3.6	3.8
总外债	13.1	12.5	11.1	8.6	8.6	9.3
外汇储备	36.6	39.8	44.3	43.5	49.2	49.6
储蓄和投资						
国内投资总额	42.1	43.0	41.7	44.0	48.2	48.8
国民储蓄	49.2	51.6	51.9	53.2	53.5	54.0
公共部门融资						
政府债务融资余额	17.8	16.2	19.6	17.0	17.7	17.0
盈余或赤字	-1.4	-0.7	0.9	-0.4	-3.1	-2.2
			(年增长率,%)			
实际有效汇率	-0.5	1.6	4.0	9.2	3.3	-0.5

数据来源:净出口、外债及国际收支数据由中国当局提供;其他数据由工作人员按历史数据估计和预测。

注:①对年度增长率的贡献度(%)。

附表4 中国金融部门的结构 (2007~2010年)

机构	2007 机构数量	2007 总资产(10亿元)	2007 占总资产的比重	2007 占GDP的比重	2008 机构数量	2008 总资产(10亿元)	2008 占总资产的比重	2008 占GDP的比重	2009 机构数量	2009 总资产(10亿元)	2009 占总资产的比重	2009 占GDP的比重	2010 机构数量	2010 总资产(10亿元)	2010 占总资产的比重	2010 占GDP的比重
银行机构	8 721	51 627	84.1	194.2	5 578	61 982	87.8	197.4	3 767	77 978	87.0	229.0	3 639	93 215	87.6	234.2
商业银行	187	40 459	65.9	152.2	323	47 819	67.8	152.3	336	61 513	68.6	180.7	379	74 160	69.7	186.3
大型商业银行	5	28 007	45.6	105.4	5	32 575	46.2	103.7	5	40 800	45.5	119.8	5	46 894	44.1	117.8
股份制商业银行	12	7 249	11.8	27.3	12	8 834	12.5	28.1	12	11 818	13.2	34.7	12	14 904	14.0	37.4
城市商业银行	124	3 340	5.4	12.6	136	4 136	5.9	13.2	143	5 680	6.3	16.7	147	7 853	7.4	19.7
农村商业银行	17	610	1.0	2.3	22	929	1.3	3.0	43	1 866	2.1	5.5	85	2 767	2.6	7.0
外国银行	29	1 252	2.0	4.7	148	1 345	1.9	4.3	133	1 349	1.5	4.0	130	1 742	1.6	4.4
本地注册的外国银行子行	…	…	…	…	32	996	1.4	3.2	38	1 132	1.3	3.3	40	1 522	1.4	3.8
外国银行的分行	…	…	…	…	116	349	0.5	1.1	95	217	0.2	0.6	90	220	0.2	0.6
政策性银行和国家开发银行	3	4 278	7.0	16.1	3	5 645	8.0	18.0	3	6 946	7.7	20.4	3	7 652	7.2	19.2
中国邮政储蓄银行	1	1 769	2.9	6.7	1	2 216	3.1	7.1	1	2 705	3.0	7.9	1	3 397	3.2	8.5
合作金融机构	8 503	5 121	8.3	19.3	5 150	6 295	8.9	20.0	3 263	6 789	7.6	19.9	2 870	7 893	7.4	19.8
农村合作银行	113	646	1.1	2.4	163	1 003	1.4	3.2	196	1 270	1.4	3.7	223	1 500	1.4	3.8
城市信用合作社①	42	131	0.2	0.5	22	80	0.1	0.3	11	27	0.0	0.1	1	2	0.0	0.0
农村信用合作社①	8 348	4 343	7.1	16.3	4 965	5 211	7.4	16.6	3 056	5 493	6.1	16.1	2 646	6 391	6.0	16.1
新型农村金融机构	27	0	0	0	101	6	0	0	164	25	0	0.1	386	113	0	0.3
村镇银行	19	0	0	0	91	6	0	0	148	25	0	0.1	349	113	0	0.3
农村互助信用合作社	8	0	0	0	10	0	0	0	16	0	0	0	37	0	0	0
非银行金融机构	690	9 744	15.9	36.7	738	8 582	12.2	27.3	772	11 666	13.0	34.3	782	13 168	12.4	33.1
保险公司	102	2 831	4.6	10.6	112	3 280	4.6	10.4	120	3 971	4.4	11.7	125	4 965	4.7	12.5
寿险公司	54	2 351	3.8	8.8	56	2 713	3.8	8.6	59	3 366	3.8	9.9	61	4 267	4.0	10.7
再保险公司①	6	89	0.1	0.3	9	101	0.1	0.3	9	116	0.1	0.3	9	115	0.1	0.3

续表

	2007				2008				2009				2010			
	机构数量	总资产(10亿元)	占总资产的比重	占GDP的比重	机构数量	总资产(10亿元)	占总资产的比重	占GDP的比重	机构数量	总资产(10亿元)	占总资产的比重	占GDP的比重	机构数量	总资产(10亿元)	占总资产的比重	占GDP的比重
非寿险公司	42	391	0.6	1.5	47	466	0.7	1.5	52	489	0.5	1.4	55	584	0.5	1.5
养老金	39	592	1.0	2.2	39	754	1.1	2.4	39	1 030	1.1	3.0	1	1 138	1.1	2.9
全国社保基金	1	440	0.7	1.7	1	562	0.8	1.8	1	777	0.9	2.3	1	857	0.8	2.2
企业年金	38	152	0.2	0.6	38	191	0.3	0.6	38	253	0.3	0.7	…	281	0.3	0.7
基金管理公司	59	3 280	5.3	12.3	61	1 939	2.7	6.2	60	2 677	3.0	7.9	63	2 520	2.4	6.3
证券投资基金②	346	3 280	5.3	12.3	439	1 939	2.7	6.2	577	2 677	3.0	7.9	704	2 520	2.4	6.3
证券公司	106	1 734	2.8	6.5	107	1 191	1.7	3.8	106	2 027	2.3	6.0	106	1 967	1.8	4.9
期货公司	177	50	0.1	0.2	171	59	0.1	0.2	167	121	0.1	0.4	164	192	0.2	0.5
合格境外机构投资者	51	286	0.5	1.1	76	179	0.3	0.6	94	290	0.3	0.9	106	297	0.3	0.7
其他非银行金融机构	152	972	1.6	3.7	168	1 181	1.7	3.8	182	1 550	1.7	4.6	213	2 089	2.0	5.2
企业集团财务公司	73	…	…	…	84	975	1.4	3.1	91	1 229	1.4	3.6	107	1 541	1.4	3.9
信托公司	54	…	…	…	54	87	0.1	0.3	58	113	0.1	0.3	63	148	0.1	0.4
金融租赁公司	10	…	…	…	12	80	0.1	0.3	12	160	0.2	0.5	17	316	0.3	0.8
货币经纪公司	2	…	…	…	3	0.1	0.0	0.0	3	0.2	0.0	0.0	4	0.3	0.0	0.0
财务公司	13	…	…	…	15	38	0.1	0.1	18	48	0.1	0.1	22	84	0.1	0.2
贷款公司	4	…	…	…	6	0	0	0	8	0	0	0	9	0.1	0.0	0
汽车金融公司③	9	…	…	…	9	38	0.1	0.1	10	48	0.1	0.1	13	84	0.1	0.2
银行业资产管理公司④	4	…	…	…	4	…	…	…	4	…	…	…	4			
整个金融体系④	9 411	61 370	100.0	230.9	6 316	70 564	100.0	224.7	4 539	89 644	100.0	263.3	4 421	106 383	100.0	267.3

数据来源：中国人民银行；中国银监会；中国证监会；中国保监会；中国国家统计局；人力资源与社会保障部。

注：①由于现有一家保险公司同时从事寿险与非寿险业务，因此，这里提供了再保险业务持有人进行管理。2007年，保险业采用了新的会计准则，适用于2007年以后的数据。

②证券投资基金的收益由基金管理公司代表基金持有人进行管理。

③表4不包括四家资产管理公司的资产。根据FSAP评估团的测算，截至2006年底，被转移到资产管理公司的不良资产账面价值大约为2.6万亿元人民币（大约占金融体系资产总额的6%，或GDP的12%）。由于2006年后资产管理公司未发布财务报告，故2007～2010年的可比数据尚未表态。

④表4未包括非正规金融，对这一块有不同的估计值。

2008年、2009年和2010年的数据由中国当局在FSAP框架下提供。2007年的数据从公开渠道收集，特别是三家监管机构的年报和全国社保基金的财务报告。有关农村与城市信用合作社的数据来源于中国银监会的年报。

附表 5　中国部分金融健康指标（2005～2010 年）[①]

	2005	2006	2007	2008	2009	2010
主要商业银行			（除另有标明外，均为百分比）			
资本充足率						
监管资本与风险加权资产的比率[②]	2.5	4.9	8.1	12.0	11.0	12.0
监管一级资本与风险加权资产的比率	…	…	6.0	9.6	8.5	9.6
减去拨备后的不良贷款与资本的比率	…	…	55.9	4.2	1.4	-2.2
资本与资产的比率[③]	4.3	5.2	5.4	5.9	5.3	6.0
资产质量						
不良贷款与贷款总额的比率	8.9	7.5	6.4	2.4	1.6	1.1
贷款损失拨备与不良贷款的比率[③]	24.8	34.3	39.2	117.9	155.4	217.7
部门贷款与贷款总额的比率[④]	…	…	97.8	97.9	99.3	…
居民	…	…	5.1	5.7	5.7	
吸收存款机构	…	…	3.0	2.1	4.2	
中央银行	…	…	1.0	1.7	1.1	
其他金融公司	…	…	0.0	0.0	0.0	
政府	…	…	70.5	69.8	68.3	
非金融公司	…	…	18.3	18.5	20.1	
其他国内部门	…	…	2.2	2.1	0.7	
收入与盈利情况						
资产收益率[②]	0.6	0.9	1.4	1.4	1.4	1.5
净资产收益率[②]	15.1	14.9	25.6	24.8	24.7	26.3
利差与总收入的比率[⑤]	…	…	83.6	81.1	78.0	79.1
非利息支出与总收入的比率[⑤]	…	…	41.2	37.0	38.4	35.5
净利差[⑤]	2.5	2.4	2.8	2.9	2.3	2.5
非利息支出与平均资产的比率[⑤]	1.7	1.7	1.6	1.8	1.4	1.4
成本与收入的比率[⑤]	46.3	51.7	39.2	38.1	41.7	36.8
利息收入与营运收入的比率[⑤]	87.4	90.2	87.7	87.1	84.8	84.2
存贷款参考利率差额[③]	333.0	360.0	333.0	306.0	306.0	306.0
流动性						
流动资产与总资产的比率	…	…	22.1	23.5	22.8	22.6
流动资产与短期负债的比率	…	…	37.6	44.7	41.6	41.2
外汇风险敞口						
外汇净头寸与资本的比率	…	…	22.7	12.8	7.4	7.4
非银行部门						
保险业						
覆盖率[⑥]	…	…	444.0	210.0	223.0	206.0
平均净资产收益率（寿险）	…	…	28.7	5.7	17.1	21.1

续表

	2005	2006	2007	2008	2009	2010
平均净资产收益率（非寿险）	…	…	-7.0	-26.2	2.9	21.5
国有企业公司部门						
国有企业的数量⑦	127 067	119 254	115 087	113 731	115 115.0	…
总债务与资本的比率	1.7	1.7	1.4	1.4	1.6	
中央政府	1.4	1.4	1.2	1.3	1.4	
地方政府	2.4	2.3	1.9	1.8	1.9	
净资产收益率	5.6	6.2	7.2	8.7	5.7	
中央政府	8.3	8.6	10.4	6.8	7.0	
地方政府	2.2	3.2	6.4	4.4	4.3	
资产收益率	2.0	2.1	3.0	3.6	2.2	
中央政府	3.2	3.2	4.8	3.0	3.0	
地方政府	0.6	0.9	2.2	1.5	1.5	
债务偿还覆盖率⑧	4.12	4.43	7.25	3.72	4.3	
中央政府	6.55	6.96	7.41	4.36	5.0	
地方政府	2.83	3.33	4.30	2.94	3.4	
中小企业						
中小企业的数量⑨	242 061	269 031	300 262	385 721	393 074	
总债务与资本的比率	1.45	1.42	1.38	1.31	1.26	
资产收益率	5.75	6.52	7.84	8.44	8.6	
净资产收益率	14.06	15.82	18.70	19.51	19.5	
债务偿还覆盖率⑧	6.47	7.09	7.33	7.43	8.64	
房地产部门						
商业房地产价格上涨率⑩	5.6	4.0	5.8	4.6	…	…
住房价格上涨率⑩	8.4	6.4	8.2	7.1	…	…
国内住房贷款占贷款总额的比率⑪	…	…	…	12.5	14.0	14.5

数据来源：中国人民银行，财政部，中国银监会，中国保监会，国务院国有资产监督管理委员会，国家统计局，国际货币基金组织《全球金融稳定报告》，Bankscope 全球银行与金融机构数据库，国际货币基金组织工作人员测算。

①除另有标明外，表 5 中的所有数据均由中国金融监管机构在 FSAP 框架下提供。以下脚注指出来源于其他公开可获得或由国际货币基金组织 FSAP 评估团测算得出的数据。

②由于覆盖面不同，跨年度数据的可比性受到限制。2005 年和 2006 年数据是指国际货币基金组织《全球金融稳定报告》中的整个银行业的数据，而 2008 年到 2010 年数据是指中国当局向 FSAP 评估团提供的 17 家主要商业银行数据。

③资本充足率和资产质量指标根据中国银监会 2010 年年报的数据计算后得出。这里将资本与资产比率定义为所有者权益与资产的比率。利差是根据中国人民银行的《货币政策执行报告》中的数据计算后得出。

④该比率的分子与分母根据国内汇总后数据计算。

⑤17 家主要商业银行的简单平均数。FSAP 评估团的计算是基于银行的财务报表和 Bankscope 全球银行与金融机构数据库。

⑥可用偿付能力与法定偿付能力额度之比。

⑦三级以上的非金融国有企业数量。国务院国有资产监督管理委员会直接持有的国有企业称为一级企业。一级国有企业直接持有的子公司称为二级企业。二级企业直接持有的子公司称为三级企业。

⑧偿还利息和缴纳税金前的盈利占利息和本金支出的百分比。

⑨工业行业中小企业的数量。

⑩商业不动产和住房价格指数的百分比变化。

⑪中国银监会根据法人机构信贷数据获得的统计。

附表6　中国金融发展指标（2005～2010年）

	2005	2006	2007	2008	2009	2010
银行业						
银行机构总数	—	19 667	8 721	5 578	3 767	3 639
分行数量/百万人口	—	140	144	146	145	146
银行存款/GDP（%）	147.2	153.3	143.5	147.5	169.6	171.3
私人信贷①/GDP（%）	114.3	113.0	111.0	108.3	129.3	131.1
银行资产/金融体系总资产（%）	—	—	84.1	87.8	87.0	87.6
银行资产/GDP（%）	197.1	198.3	194.2	197.4	229.0	234.2
保险						
寿险公司数量	42	48	54	56	59	61
非寿险公司数量	35	38	42	47	52	55
保险深度（保费占GDP的百分比）						
寿险	1.8	1.7	1.8	2.2	2.3	—
非寿险	0.9	1.0	1.1	1.0	1.1	—
保险密度（人均保费，人民币）						
寿险	250	272	336	498	554	—
非寿险	129	155	194	234	273	—
养老金						
养老金覆盖的就业人员百分比	30.1	31.5	32.8	35.4	41.2	45.7②
养老金资产/GDP（%）	1.5	1.7	2.2	2.4	3.0	2.9
养老金资产/金融体系总资产（%）	—	—	—	1.1	1.1	1.1
按揭						
按揭资产/金融体系总资产（%）	—	—	—	4.2	5.0	5.2
按揭债务存量/GDP（%）	—	—	—	9.4	13.1	14.0
货币市场						
银行间拆借（10亿元人民币）	1 278	2 150	10 647	15 049	19 350	27 868
质押式回购交易额（10亿元人民币）	15 678	26 302	44 067	56 383	67 701	84 653
买断式回购交易额（10亿元人民币）	219	292	726	1 758	2 602	2 940
中央银行票据交易额（10亿元人民币）	2 893	4 240	8 704	22 827	14 213	17 465
外汇市场						
外汇储备可用于进口的月份数	13.3	14.4	16.8	18.1	24.6	—
外汇储备/短期债务	4.8	5.4	6.5	8.6	9.3	7.6
外汇掉期交易额（10亿美元）	0	51	315	441	806	1 296
外汇远期交易额（10亿美元）	2.7	14.1	22.6	17.9	11.7	36.4

	2005	2006	2007	2008	2009	2010
资本市场						
股票市场						
上市公司数量	1 387	1 440	1 550	1 625	1 700	2 063
上市公司市值[3]/GDP（%）	17.5	41.3	123.1	38.6	71.6	66.7
股票市场交易总额/市值[3]（%）	96.4	100.4	140.8	220.1	219.7	205.6
新上市数量	15	66	124	76	99	347
新上市市值（10亿元人民币）	5.8	134.2	481.0	103.4	187.9	488.3
债券市场						
政府债券余额[4]/GDP（%）	27.3	28.9	32.4	31.3	29.3	28.1
金融债券余额/GDP（%）	10.8	12.1	12.7	13.4	15.1	15.0
公司债券余额/GDP（%）	1.7	2.6	3.0	4.1	7.1	8.6
衍生品市场						
在上海证券交易所和深圳证券交易所交易的权证总市值（10亿元人民币）	—	—	54.0	17.5	20.9	1.5
上海证券交易所和深圳证券交易所的权证年交易额（10亿元人民币）	—	—	7 783	6 969	5 365	1 499
商品期货年交易额（万亿元人民币）	—	—	20.5	36.0	65.3	113.5
人民币利率衍生品名义总额[5]（10亿元人民币）	5.0	33.3	217	529	662	1 486
人民币利率衍生品平均日交易量（10亿元人民币）	0.0	0.1	0.9	2.1	1.9	6.0
集合投资基金						
持照投资基金数量	—	—	346	439	557	704
基金管理公司数量	—	—	59	61	60	63
投资基金管理的总资产/GDP（%）	—	—	12.3	6.2	7.9	6.3
投资基金中零售投资者占比（%）	—	—	89	81	82	82
备忘：						
名义GDP（10亿元人民币）	18 494	21 631	26 581	31 405	34 051	39 798
人口（百万）	1 304	1 311	1 318	1 325	1 331	1 338

数据来源：中国人民银行，中国银监会，中国保监会，中国证监会，人力资源和社会保障部，中国外汇交易中心，国际清算银行，国际金融统计，世界发展指标，瑞士再保险公司，中国债券信息网。

①包括发放给上市企业的信贷。

②2010年的劳动力数据是估计数。

③包括在上海证券交易所和深圳证券交易所上市的公司的所有A股和B股。

④政府债券数据来自国际清算银行，包括国债和中央银行票据。

⑤中国外汇交易中心的估计值。

附表7 中国金融体系管理架构

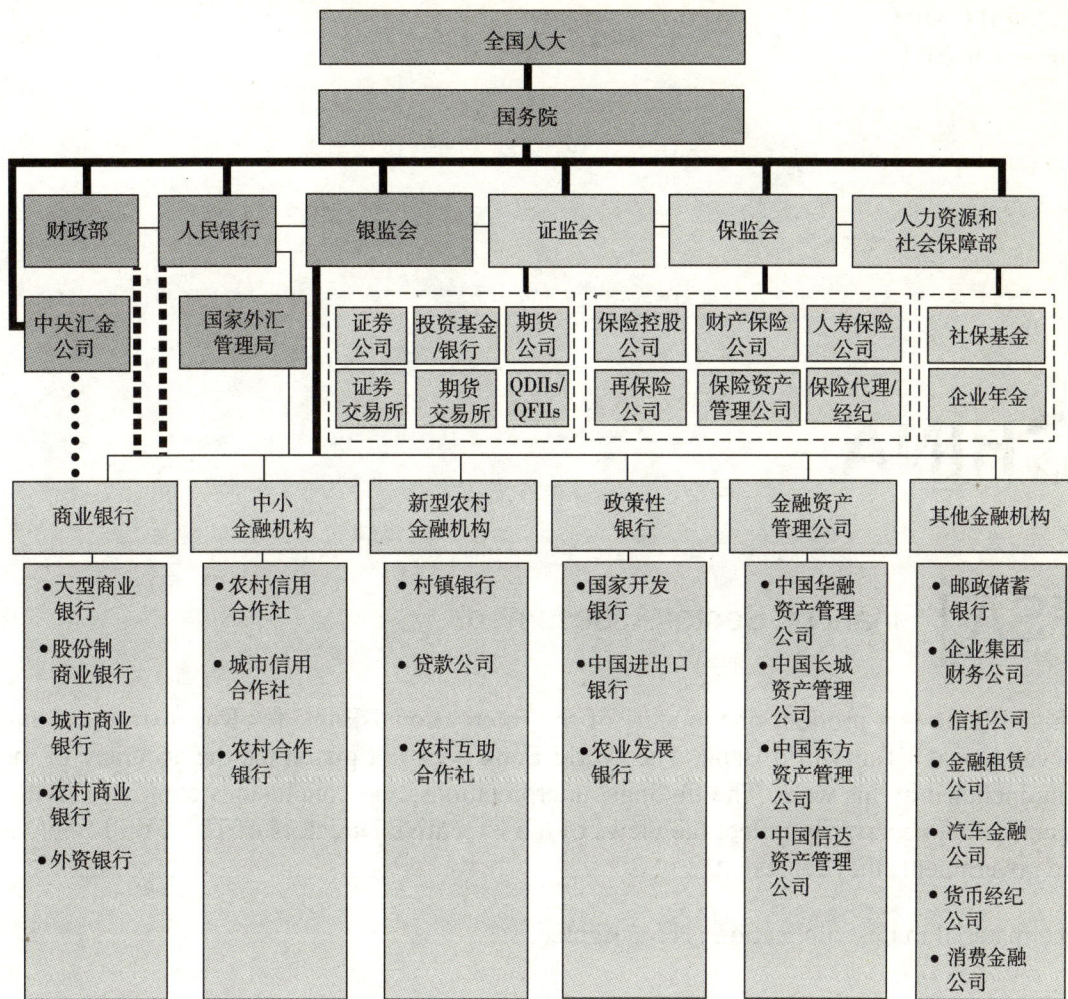

```
                          全国人大
                             │
                          国务院
                             │
   ┌──────┬──────┬──────┬──────┬──────┬──────────┐
 财政部  人民银行  银监会  证监会  保监会  人力资源和
                                              社会保障部
```

| 中央汇金公司 | 国家外汇管理局 | 证券公司 / 投资基金/银行 / 期货公司 / 证券交易所 / 期货交易所 / QDIIs/QFIIs | 保险控股公司 / 财产保险公司 / 人寿保险公司 / 再保险公司 / 保险资产管理公司 / 保险代理/经纪 | 社保基金 / 企业年金 |

商业银行	中小金融机构	新型农村金融机构	政策性银行	金融资产管理公司	其他金融机构
●大型商业银行 ●股份制商业银行 ●城市商业银行 ●农村商业银行 ●外资银行	●农村信用合作社 ●城市信用合作社 ●农村合作银行	●村镇银行 ●贷款公司 ●农村互助合作社	●国家开发银行 ●中国进出口银行 ●农业发展银行	●中国华融资产管理公司 ●中国长城资产管理公司 ●中国东方资产管理公司 ●中国信达资产管理公司	●邮政储蓄银行 ●企业集团财务公司 ●信托公司 ●金融租赁公司 ●汽车金融公司 ●货币经纪公司 ●消费金融公司

注：最粗的线代表制定金融政策的最高当局。全国人大颁布所有金融部门法律，国务院执行金融监管并对所有金融监管机构予以政策指导。点连线表示人民银行的三项主要职责：制定货币政策，维护金融稳定以及提供金融服务；同时也表示财政部作为税收管理者、财政管理者以及部分商业银行所有者的三重角色。从银监会、证监会、保监会及人力资源和社会保障部引出的较细的线表示这几家机构对各自金融部门负有监管职责。

此外，国家外汇管理局负责监管证券和保险公司的外汇业务经营。国家开发银行和邮政储蓄银行正处在向商业银行转制过程中。中央汇金公司代表国家对主要国有金融企业行使投资人的权利和义务。全国社会保障基金也具有机构投资者和部分大型商业银行持股者的双重角色。

FSAP Financial Sector Assessment Program

A joint initiative of the World Bank and the IMF

SecM2011-0492
November 2011

CHINA

FSA | Financial Sector Assessment

This volume is a product of the staff of the International Bank for Reconstruction and Development / The World Bank. The World Bank does not guarantee the accuracy of the data included in this work. The findings, interpretations, and conclusions expressed in this paper do not necessarily reflect the views of the Executive Directors of The World Bank or the governments they represent.

The material in this publication is copyrighted.

CONTENTS   **Page**

FIGURES

TABLES

Glossary

AMC	Asset Management Company	MOC	Ministry of Commerce
AML	Anti-Money Laundering	MOF	Ministry of Finance
AML/CFT	Anti-Money Laundering/Combating the Financing of Terrorism	MSEs	Micro and Small Enterprises
		MTPL	Motor Third Party Bodily Injury Insurance
CAS	Chinese Accounting Standards		
CBRC	China Banking Regulatory Commission	NBS	National Bureau of Statistics
CCDC	China Central Depositary Trust & Clearing Co., Ltd.	NDRC	National Development and Reform Commission
CCP	Central counterparty	NBFIs	Nonbank Financial Institutions
CFETS	China Foreign Exchange Trade System	NPLs	Nonperforming Loans
CIRC	China Insurance Regulatory Commission	NSSF	National Social Security Fund
		OFIs	Other Financial Institutions
CNPS	China National Payments System	PBC	People's Bank of China
CSRC	China Securities Regulatory Commission	PE	Private Equity
		PSBC	Postal Savings Bank of China
DC	Domestically Consolidated	QFIIs	Qualified Foreign Institutional Investors
EA	Enterprise Annuity	RBC	Risk-Based Capital
FATF	Financial Action Task Force	RCCs	Rural Credit Cooperatives
FHCs	Financial Holding Companies	RMB	Renminbi (yuan)
FI	Financial Intermediation	SD&C	China Securities Depository and Clearing Corporation Limited
FSAP	Financial Sector Assessment Program		
FX	Foreign Exchange	SHFE	Shanghai Futures Exchange
GEB	Growth Enterprise Board	SIFIs	Systemically Important Financial Institutions
HVPS	High Value Payments System		
IASB	International Accounting Standards Board	SIPS	Systemically Important Payment System
IBBM	Interbank Bond Market	SIVs	Structured Investment Vehicle
IFRS	International Financial Reporting Standards	SSE	Shanghai Stock Exchange
		SME	Small and Medium Enterprise
IOSCO	International Organization of Securities Commissions	SOE	State-Owned Enterprise
		SZSE	Shenzhen Stock Exchange
JSCBs	Joint-Stock Commercial Banks	WMC	Wealth Management Companies
IPOs	Initial Public Offerings	WMP	Wealth Management Products
LCBs	Large Commercial Banks	WTO	World Trade Organization
LGFP	Local Government Financing Platform	VAT	Value-Added Tax
MCCs	Micro Credit Companies	VTB	Village and Township Bank
MMMFs	Money Market Mutual Funds	ZCE	Zheng zhou Commodities Exchange

Preface

This report summarizes the findings of the Financial Sector Assessment Program (FSAP) exercise for China undertaken in 2010 by a joint IMF/World Bank team.[1] The first mission (June) assessed the observance of selected international standards and codes, and initiated discussions on a broad range of financial sector issues. The second mission (December) completed its review and presented a draft Aide-Memoire along with draft technical and background notes covering a range of topics relevant to China's financial sector.

China's financial system reform efforts have had positive results. Reforms accelerated since 2003, with the Chinese government adopting a series of policies to enhance financial sector's resilience and, on the structural side, strengthening a large part of domestic financial institutions and improving market confidence. However, risks, challenges and development opportunities remain.

This report points out near-term risks, reform challenges and development opportunities China confronts as it continues to modernize its financial sector. China faces potential vulnerabilities, near-term risks and policy-induced distortions common to an evolving financial system. The challenges and opportunities are not unique, and can be addressed. We propose that the authorities could consider carefully sequencing the following reforms and development options: (i) further deepening the commercial orientation of the financial system; (ii) moving to more market-based means of controlling monetary and financial conditions; (iii) further strengthening regulation and supervision; (iv) upgrading the framework for financial stability and crisis management; (v) revising the strategy for financial inclusion to achieve improved access to financial services ; (vi) continuing steps to support a broad based capital market; and (vii) continue to strengthen and deepen the insurance and pension sectors and (viii)continue enhancement of the financial market infrastructure.

Addressing the opportunities and challenges will require creative thinking and a willingness to change. A gradualist and piece-meal approach to financial sector reforms likely will fall short in meeting the increasing depth and complexity of China's financial market. Going forward it will be important to have a holistic approach and to look beyond current laws and regulations for potential means to address market changes as well as to find solutions to current inhibiting factors preventing the attainment of Government goals.

---

[1] Jonathan Fiechter (IMF, Mission Co-Chief), Thomas A. Rose (World Bank, Mission Co-Chief), Udaibir S. Das (Deputy Mission Chief, IMF), Mario Guadamillas (Deputy Mission Chief, World Bank), Massimo Cirasino, Patrick Conroy, Asli Demirgüç-Kunt, Catiana Garcia-Kilroy, Haocong Ren, Heinz Rudolph, Jun Wang, Ying Wang, Luan Zhao (all World Bank); César Arias, Martin Čihák, Silvia Iorgova, Yinqiu Lu, Aditya Narain, Nathan Porter, Shaun Roache, Tao Sun, Murtaza Syed (all IMF); Nuno Cassola, Henning Göbel, Keith Hall, Nick Le Pan, Rodney Lester, Greg Tanzer, Nancy Wentzler, and Walter Yao (all experts).

The mission met senior officials from the China FSAP Taskforce comprised of the Ministry of Foreign Affairs, National Development and Reform Commission (NDRC), the Ministry of Finance (MOF), the Ministry of Human Resources and Social Security, the Ministry of Commerce, People's Bank of China (PBC), National Bureau of Statistics (NBS), Legislative Affairs Office of the State Council, China Banking Regulatory Commission (CBRC), China Securities Regulatory Commission (CSRC), China Insurance Regulatory Commission (CIRC), State Administration of Foreign Exchange (SAFE), and other ministries and agencies including the Ministry of Industry and Information Technology, the Ministry of Housing and Urban-Rural Development, the Ministry of Agriculture, National Audit Office, State-Owned Assets Supervision and Administration Commission of the tate Council, State Administration of Taxation and National Council for Social Security Fund, and staff from these agencies, as well as representatives from financial institutions, industry Organizations, and private sector representatives in Beijing, Chongqing, Guangzhou, Nanchang, Ningbo, Shanghai, and Shenzhen.

The team would like to convey its deep appreciation to the Chinese authorities and other counterparts for their hospitality, technical engagement, and generous support in facilitating its work.

Overall Assessment and Recommendations

1. China's financial system reforms are progressing well. The authorities are seeking to shift the financial sector from a centrally directed system to one that is commercially-based and financially sound. Improvements are seen in the structure, performance, and oversight of the financial sector. The system is becoming more transparent as it opens up.

2. China is confronted by a build-up of potential sources of vulnerabilities, including greater exposure to external shocks. The inter-linkages across markets and institutions are growing, and de-facto banks and informal credit markets, conglomerate structures, and off-balance sheet activities are on the rise. The reform of small-and medium-sized rural financial institutions continues. There is a need for close monitoring, better data collection, intensive information exchange and a stronger framework for identifying and addressing problem institutions and market practices that could impair the on-going reformprocess.

3. The near term domestic risks are four-fold: (i) the impact of the recent sharp credit expansion on banks' asset quality; (ii) the rise of off-balance sheet exposures and lending outside the formal banking sector; (iii) the relatively high level of real estate and commodity prices; and (iv) the increase of imbalances due to the current economic growth pattern. Stress tests of 17 commercial banks suggest that most major banks are resilient to risk in isolation, but gaps and weaknesses in the informational infrastructure make it difficult to assess the possible transmission effect through the economic and financial system. There is potential for damage to financial stability and continued reform should the risks arise simultaneously.

4. Macroeconomic and financial policies need to be better aligned to create incentives for a durable transformation to a more commercially oriented and effective financial system. Emphasis should be on credit allocation processes, financial markets and services that reduce the need for high levels of precautionary savings, and more resilient and transparent institutional structures. To facilitate this process, the government should continue to reorient its role and responsibilities. The state's involvement in financial markets and institutions—through ownership of banks and state owned enterprises, management of interest rates, setting of priorities for the financial system, and as an implicit guarantor—is resulting in moral hazard, weak risk management in banks, and a buildup of contingent risk and liabilities.

5. The commercialization of the financial system needs deepening. Credit risk strategies are dominated by loan growth targets. The use of commercial bank credit for policy goals should be replaced by other mechanisms such as direct fiscal expenditures, government credit programs and rationalization of policy banks. Bank risk management and supervisory assessments focus too much on backward-looking variables and not enough on forward-looking assessments of credit risk. The concentration of bank exposures to state owned enterprises, the guaranteed margins, the limited ability and willingness to differentiate loan rates, as well as the implicit guidance on credit flows, undermine the development of effective credit risk management capabilities at banks. In this context, a move to more market-based means of controlling monetary and financial conditions would greatly improve credit allocation. Market interest rates should become the primary instrument for managing credit expansion.

6. Continued advances in the regulatory and supervisory regime are required. Efforts are needed to implement consolidated supervision and ensure timely sharing of essential information among all relevant government bodies. The PBC and the primary supervisory commissions must be empowered and have resources commensurate with their expanding responsibilities. The mandates of the supervisory commissions should focus on ensuring safety and soundness of regulated institutions and proper market conduct. Approaches to supervision should be more forward looking in lieu of issuing large quantities of regulations and using very detailed approval processes for governing the day-to-day activities of financial institutions. In addition, customers of financial products and services must be made aware of the underlying risks and obligations through improved market disclosure and enhanced financial literacy. To support this, improvements in accounting requirements, data standards, reporting requirements, and meaningful disclosure are necessary.

7. A formalized stability framework to monitor and respond to macro-financial vulnerabilities would benefit China. Building on the experience from the ad-hoc committee in place since June 2008, a permanent Financial Stability Committee should be established having access to relevant supervisory and other financial information.

8. A framework to resolve weak financial institutions on a timely basis is needed. The framework should assist in resolving distressed financial institutions at least cost to the public, and facilitate the wind up of institutions in an orderly manner. To facilitate this and to protect the PBC's balance sheet, a deposit insurance fund could be established to finance the orderly resolution of failed institutions and to protect insured depositors. A government entity should be vested with authority to monitor the health of the financial system and have resolution powers for dealing with institutions declared nonviable by their supervisors.

9. Broader and more diversified financial products and services would deepen and strengthen China's financial system. Interdependencies between the government and the corporate fixed income markets and policies relating to the interest rate regime should be considered. This should include: (i) a more proactive government debt issuance strategy to support the risk-free yield curve; (ii) expanding access to new non-government issuers; and (iii) increasing the supply of different types of instruments to address the diverse needs of issuers and investors. This should be accompanied by improvements to the repo markets; developing risk pooling and hedging products; prudently promoting the development of securitization, and measures to ensure regulatory consistency across all types of fixed income products.

10. Financial infrastructure and relevant legal systems need to be further upgraded. Progress has been seen, but more is needed to: a) enhance the legal framework and oversight function of the payments and securities settlement system, b) improve the coverage and quality of the Credit Reference Center, c) improve the oversight and quality of credit rating agencies, d) upgrade and strengthen consumer protection, e) enhance the insolvency regime and creditors rights; f) define a clear process for dealing with troubled financial institutions and depositors and g) establish a framework and tools for effective macro prudential and financial stability.

11. Financial Inclusion could be enhanced through a revised strategy. This should include reforms to provide the right incentives for: provision of financial services to under-served sectors; market competition and contestability (by adjusting entry and exit criteria); improving the legal framework for financial inclusion; and removing policies not properly aligned with the overall objective of improving access.

12. Sequencing reforms at the appropriate pace will be a challenge, but essential to China's sustained growth. This will be crucial to maintaining a balance between development and financial stability while minimizing risks. To facilitate the process, a prioritized list of key recommendations needing consideration was provided (Table 1).

I. Structure and Functioning of the Financial System

A. Context

1. China's progress in reforming and developing its financial system has been considerable (Table 2). This development has been supported by key banking sector reforms, creation of capital markets, introduction of a prudential regulatory regime, bank recapitalizations, and a broad-based opening of the financial system following accession to the WTO and reforms since 2003. Joint-stock reforms—including initial government capital injections, and subsequent strategic investor participation and initial public offerings (IPOs) have boosted large banks' commercial orientation. Banks have diversified their equity structures; enhanced corporate governance; introduced internal controls and risk management; and increasingly adopted profit-maximizing strategies. Key securities companies were restructured, and a securities companies' resolution mechanism and an investor protection scheme set up. Insurance sector reform also progressed.

2. The reform of financial policy is underway but distortions remain. These are linked to remaining interest rate policies, quantitative credit guidance, limited investment channels, and moral hazard related to the perception of implicit state guarantees. As a result, China's system is characterized by: (i) a low cost of capital that does not remunerate adequately domestic households; (ii) a propensity for prices to deviate from market clearing levels; (iii) inadequate incentives to price risk in view of the implicit guarantees on large state-owned enterprise (SOEs)' debt;[2] (iv) emphasis on minimizing NPLs on balance sheets; (v) high levels of structural liquidity; (vi) incentives to push credit off-balance sheet; and (vii) still limited non-state ownership— including foreign shareholder participation—in the financial system. Direct allocation and credit pricing facilitated China's strong growth, when sectors with high-growth potential were easily identified, but they also contributed to overcapacity, potential asset bubbles, and the need for public-funded bank recapitalizations.

3. Credit is primarily channeled via the banking system, with a limited role for domestic capital markets (Figure 1). At end-2009, commercial bank loans accounted for a larger share of total financial system assets compared to others. Nonbank financial institutions (NBFIs)—including trust investment companies, financial leasing companies, and finance companies—have been growing (Table 4).

4. The state of development of the financial sector can be seen in the high degree of

---

[2] Lending ceilings have been removed, but banks do not let lending rates float up from benchmarks, reflecting incentives to lend to safer borrowers (supported by implicit guarantees), and an insufficient ability to price risks.

Figure 1. China: Size of Selected Countries' Financial Systems, 2009

(In percent of total)

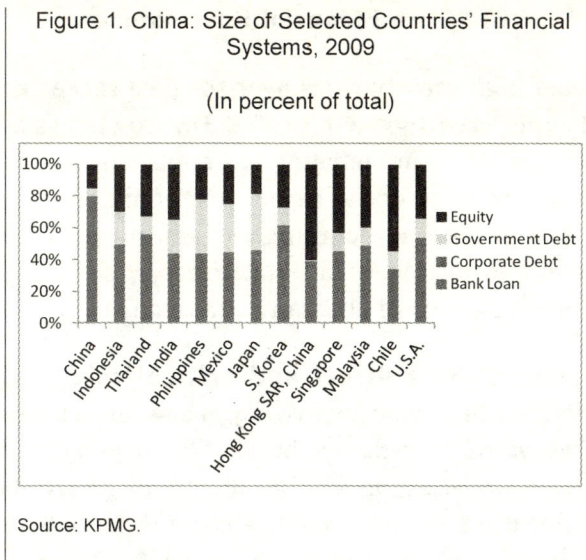

Source: KPMG.

bank savings deposits given limited alternative investment options (Figure 2). Deposits account for over 80 percent of banking system liabilities and have grown by an average of 19 percent. Recently, corporate deposits have become a principal driver of bank funding growth due to strong corporate profitability and household deposits have shifted reflecting an increased risk appetite and low deposit rates.

Figure 2. China: Levels and Incremental Growth of Bank Deposits

(In trillions of RMB)

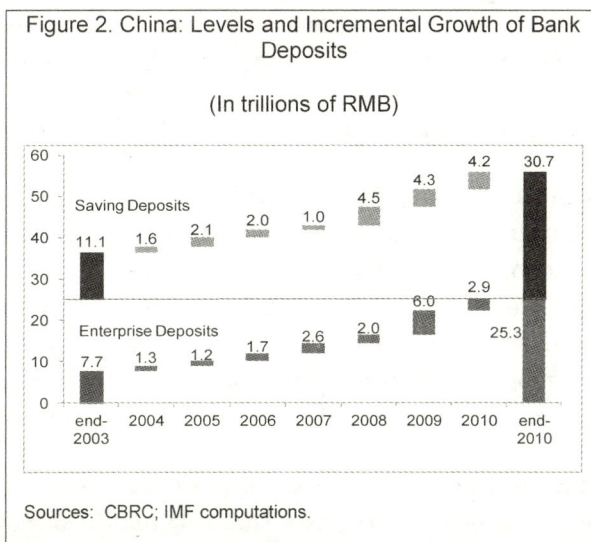

Sources: CBRC; IMF computations.

B. Macro-Financial Environment

5. China has maintained high growth rates over the past three decades, on the back of high investment and rapid credit growth (Table 3). Growth has averaged double-digits since the start of reforms in 1978, and inflation has remained relatively subdued reflecting rapid productivity growth and additions to capacity from high levels of investment. Public debt remains low, although there are contingent liabilities. The economy is prone to asset bubbles, notably in the stock and real estate market, given high levels of structural liquidity, low interest rates, and lack of alternative investment vehicles.

6. The financial system plays a direct and critical role in the transmission of macroeconomic policies. In China there are five key macro-financial linkages: i) *The banking system directly facilitates quasi-fiscal policy* through its use as a credit channel; ii) *Banking system directly facilitates monetary policy*, but the credit growth targets undermine the efficiency of credit allocation; iii) *Low cost of capital distorts the saving-investment balance of the economy*; iv) *Capital markets' underdevelopment limits alternatives for corporate funding and household investments*, and represents an impediment to solving structural problems in the financial sector: low rates of return on savings; high precautionary savings through banks; high savings by private enterprises without access to capital markets; continued bank-dominance of the financial system; and potential asset bubbles; v) *Lack of contestability of markets or ownership for large firms limits competition*.

C. The Regulatory and Supervisory Framework

7. Progress has been made to improve financial regulation and supervision, but the challenge is to increase its efficacy, quality, and responsiveness. The FSAP revealed a high degree of adherence to international standards. However, going forward, the right balance must be struck between the degree of regulatory control and the need to enable useful innovation and development of the financial system. Suggestions arising out of the assessment were to improve: i) the operational autonomy of supervisory commissions, ii) skills, iii) risk monitoring capabilities, iv) resources and v) interagency coordination.

8. Commercial Bank Regulation and Supervision

    a. CBRC has made strides in improving its framework for supervising commercial banks. It has a clear safety and soundness mandate but its operational autonomy is challenged by the continued use of the state dominated banking system to pursue development goals and rapid credit growth. Going forward, it will be important to ensure its ability to act fully in pursuit of its mandate. This should include adequate budget and supervisory resources so it can respond to the increasing scale and complexity of the Chinese banking sector.

    b. Banking legal and regulatory framework has been brought in line with international standards, but gaps remain. Identified gaps: a) absence of a requirement to be informed of changes in indirect control and the identification of banks beneficial owners and clients; b) inadequate rules on related parties and c) lack of a legal framework underpinning bank resolution.

9. Securities Intermediaries and Securities Market Regulation

a. **The CSRC has overseen regulatory reforms to support a more market-based financial system.** A credible program of inspection and surveillance is in place but a stronger emphasis is needed on illegal investment activities and monitoring of hedge funds and private equity(PE) funds. Steps have been taken for detecting and deterring insider trades and market manipulation, but more is needed. CSRC should introduce a formal on-site inspection program of the exchanges to bolster oversight and it should implement and strengthen monitoring of risk-based net capital rules and "Know your client" rules.

b. **The legal and regulatory framework for the regulation of securities markets needs to be further improved to keep pace with market developments.** Areas for improvement include the commercial court, enforcement with respect to illegal investment activities and detection and deterrence of unfair trading practices. CSRC needs greater operational autonomy to enable it to more effectively carry out its mandate without the potential for interference. Budget flexibility is needed so it can respond to the rapid growth of markets and the limited role played by market discipline. The accounting and auditing profession has made strides, but there is a need to continue to develop its size and expertise to meet the increasing size and growing complexity of the market.

10. Insurance Regulations and Supervision

a. **CIRC has a comprehensive supervisory framework, with emphasis on corporate governance rules , consumer protection efforts and risk management systems, though improvements are needed in:** i) off-site monitoring through reinstatement of early warning ratios; ii) the non-life liability and solvency regimes; iii) the life minimum solvency margin to make it more risk based as investment options are expanded; iv) ensuring explicit and clear regulation for facilitating the exit of insurance companies from the market via run off or portfolio transfers and v) the coordination and exchange of information between PBC and CIRC in the area of AML. In addition, strict measures should be taken to prevent insurance companies operating below the 100 percent solvency level from issuing new business.

b. **The CIRC's mandate and operational autonomy need to be addressed.** The developmental mandate for CIRC should be reviewed to ensure it can focus on its real mandate. Its budget should ensure adequate organizational and industry capacity. The current prescriptive, rules-based system should be reconsidered as the market and the risk-based supervisory regime mature.

11. Regulation of Other Financial Institutions

a. **Regulation of other financial institutions (OFIs) aims to ensure their link with the formal banking sector remains limited.** In addition to commercial and policy banks, there are a host of other NBFIs which are part of the credit delivery system. Some trust companies, finance companies of enterprise groups, and leasing companies, etc., are regulated by the CBRC. In addition, there are entities in the informal financial sector (pawn shops, financing guarantee institutions, micro-finance companies, etc.) which are licensed by local governments and unregulated entities (informal banks) which are surveyed or investigated by the PBC occasionally.

b. **Regulatory policies applied to shadow banks and their responsibilities need to be clarified.** CBRC and NDRC view the universe of shadow banks as comprising mainly PE(the majority of which have not been regulated) and informal lenders and deposit takers (monitored by the PBC and CBRC). The regulatory policies applying to shadow banks and their responsibilities need to be clarified. Interagency coordination backed by memoranda of understanding for information sharing, needs to be strengthened to prevent episodes of build-up of systemic risk via cross-market financial products or activities.

II. The Banking Sector

12. The banking system is dominated by large commercial banks (LCBs) and joint-stock commercial banks (JSCBs). Collectively, the five LCBs and the twelve JSCBs accounted for 83 percent of total commercial bank assets at end-2010 (Figure 3). All LCBs and most JSCBs are owned or partially owned by the government and thus, most are substantially controlled by the government. Deepening the commercial orientation of the banking sector will serve to foster a general deepening of the entire financial sector.

13. The banking sector balance sheets have expanded rapidly in part due to the macroeconomic stimulus policies. As a result credit demand for infrastructure and transportation increased. A large proportion of such demand came through local government financing platforms (LGFPs) that have increased considerably as a result of the 2009 economic stimulus. The fiscal revenue and expenditure mismatches coupled with the inability of local governments to borrow directly have made it difficult to achieve appropriate balance between rapid economic growth and avoiding undue financial risks.

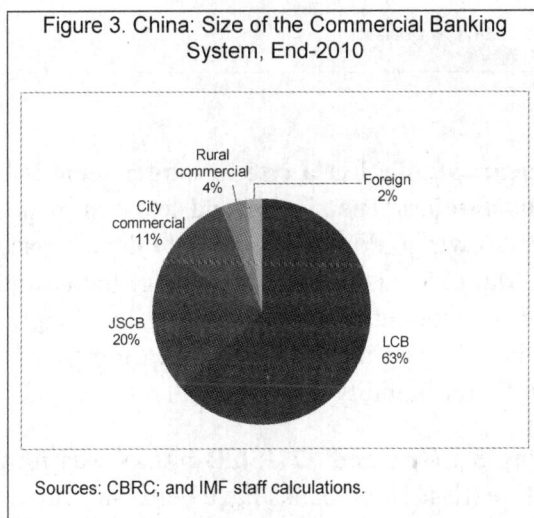

Figure 3. China: Size of the Commercial Banking System, End-2010

Sources: CBRC; and IMF staff calculations.

14. Banking sector profits remained high as a result of large expansion of credit and balance sheets, in part due to the macroeconomic stimulus policies. A large portion of the demand came from local governments. This, together with the credit demand for property purchases and credit creation associated with large FX inflows, led to a surge of new RMB loans. In addition, off-balance sheet exposures have expanded rapidly since the Q2 of 2009, mostly as a result of banks' promoting wealth-management products.

15. Banks' NPL ratios reflect a downward trend, reaching 1.1 percent at end-2010 (Figure 4). This decline was driven by rapid expansion of credit and the significant decline in NPLs. The contraction of NPLs to RMB 434 billion at end-2010 from RMB 1.3 trillion at end-2005 substantially reflects the carve-out and resolution of RMB 816 billion (NPLs) from one large bank in 2008. The migration of some loans to performing status and some improvements in risk management in banks also has prevented NPL levels from rising

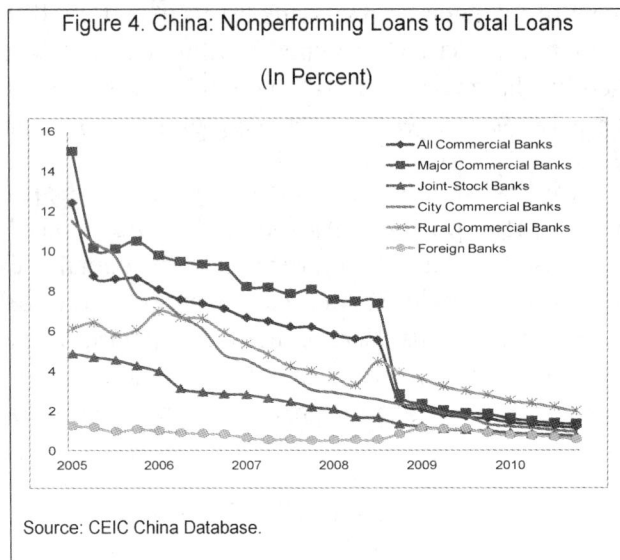

Figure 4. China: Nonperforming Loans to Total Loans

(In Percent)

Source: CEIC China Database.

16. Banks' funding appears stable, but a rise in longer-term loans adds to challenges for banks' maturity mismatches. The sizable and low-cost deposit base contributed to stable bank funding. The growth in domestic corporate deposits since 2008 has become a driver of total deposits. Maturity mismatches are rising. Increasing reliance on medium- and long-term loans for investment project financing has lengthened asset maturities. Interest rate mismatch is balanced by the regular repricing of loans, but the maturity mismatches pose challenges for liquidity management.

17. A stress test covering 5 LCBs and 12 JSCB banks was jointly conducted by the FSAP team and the authorities. These banks have better information disclosure and more sophisticated risk management systems than other banks. The exercise was done in close cooperation with the PBC and CBRC. It involved single-factor shocks and macroeconomic scenario analysis, but was limited by the lack of consistent data. The shock sizes took into account past experience in China and other countries, as well as past FSAP practice. The single-factor sensitivity calculations suggest that the system would be able to withstand a range of sector-specific shocks occurring in isolation. The analysis suggests that the system could be severely impacted if several major shocks materialized concurrently.

III. Strengthening Bond and Equity Markets

18. The capital market as an alternative funding channel to banks has grown over the last five years (Table 6), but an enourmous potential for growth remains untapped. Although progress has been seen in establishing a multilayer capital market addresing finanical needs of both large or state-owned enterprises with high credit ratings and SMEs. However, there is still room for a more relevant role of capital markets as a funding source for large enterprises with lower credit ratings (even above investment grade) and SMEs. Bank dominance in the financial sector presents challenges in developing the capital markets as an effective capital raising mechanism.

19. Despite prospects of banking disintermediation deepening, the banking sector is expected to continue playing a prominent role in capital market development. As issuers, underwriters, distributors, investors and liquidity providers, banks would influence the speed and quality of growth of fixed income markets. The speed of development of the market also will be influenced by Government's plans for further interest rate reform.

20. A full-fledged Government bond market is needed for the growth of diversified and sophisticated fixed income markets. Currently the risk-free yield curve is unevenly developed as the Government shares it with PBC bills in the short term and the more liquid Policy Bank bonds in the medium term (Figure 5). While the active use of PBC bills has thus far played an important role in setting up the basis and infrastructure for further development of a fully fledged bond market, going forward the continued issuance in sizeable volumes of these bills may require further institutional coordination with the MOF on its issuance policy of instruments of similar maturities. This is a common evolution observed in many advanced emerging market economies that are confronted to large sterilization needs related to capital inflows as they pursue development of a liquid risk free yield curve. It is expected that as China's economy continues to progress such disparities will be mitigated as large sterilization needs diminish with reduced capital inflows.

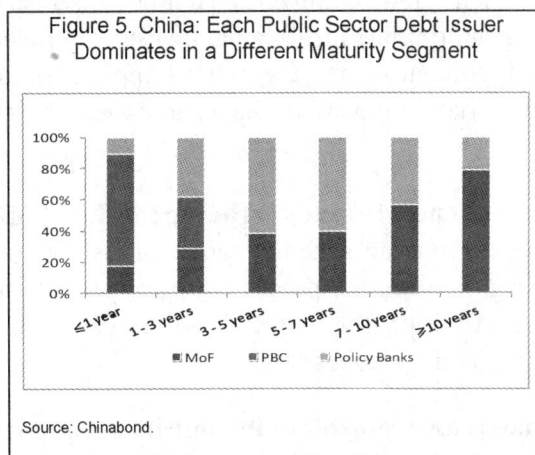

Figure 5. China: Each Public Sector Debt Issuer Dominates in a Different Maturity Segment

Source: Chinabond.

21. A more proactive and sustained benchmark building strategy is required. This should include strengthening of coordination between the MOF and the PBC in common maturities and active liability management to support benchmark building. This would help to provide clarity to market participants, support secondary market liquidity and the development of interest rate hedging instruments while increasing bond market development.

22. Currently, regulatory oversight of China's fixed income markets involves three agencies (PBC, NDRC and CSRC). Their respective roles should be further clarified to ensure regulations are consistent and equivalent regulations apply to similar types of participants even if regulators are different. A possible option would be to delineate regulatory responsibilities between the wholesale and retail markets which would be supportive of existing market practices, but regulatory consistency should be strengthened and connectivity improved (between the Interbank and the Exchange fixed income markets). Alternatively, other models may be followed which could accomplish this desired result.

23. In promoting the development of sub-national debt markets, it will be important to carefully account for associated risks and to ensure timely public disclosure of data. This is key to ensuring risks do not get transferred as contingent liability to the government and do not negatively impact the development of the fixed income market. It will be important that provincial issuers have technical capacity to issue and manage debt and periodically undertake debt sustainability analysis. Also, it will be vital to ensure that investors are diversified and that the commercial banking system is not a captive investor.

24. More is needed for the development of a segment of the fixed income market that accommodates lower, yet credible, credit rating standards. This will allow SMEs and other private enterprises to access these markets. Innovations in relation to SMEs launched over the past year appear to be supportive of market development. Concern of the authorities in managing risks associated with the entry of enterprises with lower credit standings is legitimate, but a more flexible approach would enable the creation of a segment of eligible investment grade companies. Action would be required on the supply and demand side, to enable appropriate institutional investors to invest in these instruments. In addition, easing the 40 percent of net assets limit applicable to corporation's market based debt issuance should have a positive impact in expanding direct funding capacity instead of bank funding.

25. Opportunities to further improve the Inter-Bank Bond Market exist. Enhancements to the market making scheme, such as those contemplated by MOF and PBC are a critical building block in the process of price formation and the development of a risk-free yield curve. Additionally, market liquidity can be expected to improve by further leveling the playing field for nonbank participants.

26. The repo market has grown substantially, but its economic impact is limited by legal and operational constraints. The dominance of pledged repos and the limited use of documented outright repos enabling collateral re-hypothecation, limits liquidity and necessary linkages between money markets and Government bond markets. In a market as large as China's, the volume of documented outright repos is unusually small which has led to the development of an informal repo market. Formalizing and standardizing the former is critical to the efficiency and integrity of fixed income markets.

27. The underdevelopment of effective hedging instruments, such as interest rate derivatives, is an additional obstacle to the further development of the capital market. The low liquidity of government debt limits its development. Upgrades in the government issuance policy, secondary market organization and repos would provide a sound framework to build derivatives markets.

28. China's equity markets have evolved, but challenges remain. One challenge involves reinforcing the role of the Shanghai Stock Exchange (SSE) as a relevant source of funding for large enterprises other than SOEs. Technological and regulatory initiatives and investments have been made, however, other challenges remain such as increasing the current low percentage of free float among public companies and SOEs. A second challenge involves better serving the financing needs of SMEs. The implementation of a multitier market system in the Shenzhen Stock Exchange comprising the Main Board, the SME Board (2004) and the Growth Enterprise Board (GEB) (2009) seems to be a step in the right direction and going forward should contribute to the further expansion of cost effective funding for a broad spectrum of enterprises.

29. It is critical for China's capital markets that regulators of the different types of institutional investors (mutual funds, pension funds, insurance companies) have a concerted strategy to develop a diversified institutional investor base. A stronger presence of institutions would increase efficiency in the allocation of capital, support the expansion of listings and listed shares, and reduce volatility. In fixed income markets, a more flexible approach to investments, within prudent limits, would enhance access to a large segment of private companies that would still be within investment grade credit ratings.

30. Developing a sound investor base is challenging and requires, among others: a more active role of banks in the growth of institutional investors as owners of AMCs and distributors; ensuring that regulations of collective investment pools are consistent with the expansion of capital markets to private enterprises; and monitoring regulatory arbitrage opportunities emerging in the context of the fast growing WMCs.

IV. Developing A Sound Insurance Sector

31. The insurance sector has grown rapidly, but has scope for further deepening. Its assets under management corresponded to less than 11 percent of China's domestic personal bank deposits at end-2009. The sector is already the six largest in the world, reflecting China's enormous population and the fact that its life (personal lines) sector is sizeable. But there is further scope for deepening. In particular, penetration in the non life (property & casualty) sector is lower than expected given income levels and structural metrics.

32. The rapid growth has been associated with important risks. Insurance companies have seen growth rates of real premiums above 15 percent per annum, and these are expected to be sustained in the near future. At the same time, returns to equity in the non life sector have not been sufficient on average to sustain capital growth adequate to fund the commensurate rates of increase in the basic risk elements.

33. Most of the 87 insurers licensed in the current decade continue to lose money under the current accounting methodology. In many cases this reflects establishment costs and rapid growth, with economic values (based on future cash flows) actually increasing. However a number of insurers have fallen below, or close to, the 100 percent solvency level and CIRC will need to monitor these closely in case their business models prove to be defective. Rapid expansion (typically through highly competitive commissions and pricing) is also placing profit pressures on larger established insurers. While the great majority of insurers meet current minimum solvency requirements the aggregate solvency position could be strengthened. The current distribution of solvency ratios adds considerably to CIRC's supervisory load, and potentially also has negative development implications.

34. Recent steps by CIRC appear to have been effective in stabilizing the technical results of the non life sector. Actions taken to deal with capital requirements include raising capital by listing the major insurers (most of which are state and provincially controlled), allowing generous levels of proportional reinsurance, allowing approved insurers to issue subordinated debt and include this for statutory solvency determination, and adopting forbearance in certain cases. Solvency standards have been the subject of research and review within CIRC and it is desirable that strengthened prudential standards are expedited, particularly in the life sector as investment options are expanded.

35. A rationalization strategy is needed and could be fostered by introducing more comprehensive Risk Based Capital (RBC) requirements and requiring shareholders to achieve these over a suitable period. Strengthening the actuarial oversight of non life claims provisioning and clarifying the voluntary wind up and exit rules and processes are also desirable steps. In addition, other strategies could involve taking action to enable insurers to generate more stable and higher returns to equity. This could include placing motor third party bodily injury insurance (MTPL) in a central mutual pool(s) to be anaged separately by approved insurers, introducing pricing that is more reflective of underlying risks and similarly developing properly priced (possibly subsidized) catastrophe insurance pools.

36. A further desirable prudential step is to require assets matching life insurance mathematical reserves and minimum capital requirements to be explicitly earmarked and not available as collateral for borrowing (although approved repos could be allowed to enhance yields as long as possession of the underlying asset is retained). The fact that staff salaries and benefits and secured borrowers rank ahead of life policyholders in the event of a wind up is contrary to international best practice.

37. A number of governance items with prudential implications should be reviewed. Related party transactions are permitted and while these are subject to governance regulations, the rules are not sufficiently precise to prevent malfeasance. As insurance groups and financial conglomerates become more common, all related party transactions above a certain size plus loans to management/staff should require CIRC clearance and then be reported in the annual accounts.

V. Addressing Challenges in the Pension Sector

38. China is gradually consolidated its multi-pillar pension system, but it is facing sizable challenges. The Old Age Insurance System (first pillar) includes an unfunded and a partially funded component. The second pillar, or enterprise annuity (EA) system, is a voluntary occupational supplementary pension system. The third pillar includes personal and occupational pension plans that offer greater flexibility than the EA system, but have been largely unexploited. Each of the pillars faces challenges that require the attention of the authorities.

39. Pension reserves of the first pillar are invested in inefficient portfolios. Tier 1 of the first pillar is a traditional unfunded pay-as-you-go system. Tier 2 of the first pillar is a partially funded system with individual accounts, managed by the government. Due to a lack of sufficient funds to finance the transition to a fully funded system, many local governments financed the shortage of Tier 1 with resources of the individual accounts. Among the provinces with Tier 2 backed by real assets, most of the pension resources are invested in low earning bank deposits and short-term bills. Nine provinces have part of their Tier 2 pension assets (central government subsidies on personal accounts) managed by the National Social Security Fund (NSSF), which is a model that can be replicated across the country.

40. Better pension funds investment strategies are essential for fostering the development of the capital market. Capital protections investment strategies, which are common across pension funds, will not be sufficient for obtaining reasonable pensions in the future. Longer-term horizon strategies involving equity and long term bonds will be necessary. Investment regulation should discourage short term evaluation of performance and focus on aligning the investment strategies with the long term objectives of the contributors.

41. The EA covers mostly workers of state owned companies. Limited tax benefits, a complex design of the EA governance framework, and an incomplete regulatory structure have been impediments to the development of the EA system. Since the regulatory framework of EA system is not compatible with the structure of labor agreements of SMEs and the weak enforcement of the labor contracts, it is unlikely the EA system will grow at the necessary speed to cope with the growth of employment in urban areas.

42. An option for consideration given China's savings culture is to foster the development of personal pension plans. This idea would channel part of precautionary savings into retirement savings. There is room for designing personal income tax incentives[3] for the contributions and matching fund contributions (for lower income individuals) to incentive retirement savings individual accounts. These initiatives could provide coverage to a large segment of the population that currently does not have formal retirement savings plans. Personal pension plans could offer standardized pension products consistent with the long term objectives of contributors. Although different institutions would be allowed to offer different products, the investment strategy of the plans should be aligned with a portfolio benchmark designed by independent experts following the life cycle approach.

---

[3] The current structure of the personal income tax system which separates sources of income, rather than treating income as a whole, makes crafting the incentive more challenging. Care should be taken to ensure the targeted group will be the ones best positioned to take advantage of the incentive. Since they are not covered today by any formal pension system, perhaps the incentive could be structured to apply to only those with no formal coverage today.

VI. Policy and Strategic Issues in Promoting Inclusive Finance

43. **Progress has been made in financial services that depend on extensive networks and technical advancements, but access remains limited for rural and urban households, micro and small businesses.** Demand for credit by rural households is, to some extent, met by informal providers. Alternative financial services such as non-life insurance, factoring and leasing are still at their nascent stages.

44. **China has a huge potential to develop greater financial inclusion.** To meet this potential, the following should be considered: i) further reform of financial institutions to bring out their potential in delivering financial services and products to the most productive users, ii) reform of the roles and functions of government in the provision of finance, and iii) further improvements to the financial infrastructure and regulatory oversight.

45. **To build an integrated and coherent rural and MSE finance strategy, further improvements are needed.** As a result of rapid urbanization and industrialization and demographic movements, commercial sustainability in rural and micro finance has shifted and the need for policy-oriented financial services has reduced. A policy, based upon the objective of promoting convenient, speedy and long-lasting access to financial services and products based on commercial principles is needed. The primary role of government should be to provide an environment and infrastructure in which well-governed and supervised financial institutions compete with each other in serving rural and MSE clients. There is a need to clarify the roles and functions of government agencies and more could be done in promoting regulatory effectiveness in the area of inclusive finance.[4] The remaining restrictions and obstacles in rural and MSE finance (in the areas of market entry, funding, geographic expansion and mobile banking) should be carefully reviewed.

46. **The potential role of financial institutions in broadening access should be further explored.** Many banks have embarked on the path of commercially oriented lending to rural households and MSEs. The emerging rural financial institutions—Village and Township Bank (VTB), lending companies and rural mutual cooperatives — and Micro Credit Companies (MCCs) have exerted some competitive pressure but their role will take time to develop. To further broaden outreach there is a need to further strengthen some state-owned financial institutions—especially the Agricultural Development Bank of China (ADBC) and PSBC—and the RCCs, to enable them to further improve their corporate governance and risk management.

---

[4] All told there are over a dozen types of financial institutions that are registered locally, subject to minimum or no regulation and supervision.

47. To create a framework for inclusive finance, the authorities should consider legislative and other changes. This should focus on: (1) expanded consumer credit information coverage; (2) a national secured transaction framework and out of court settlements; (3) developing factoring and leasing as alternative means of finance for the MSEs; (4) rules for the existence and business conduct of informal lenders; (5) careful performance evaluation of policy lending programs and (6) designing a statistical system to place emphasis on true outreach (measured by the number of micro loans and clients), efficiency, and financial sustainability.

48. Continued liberalization of lending interest rates is essential to commercially sustainable rural and MSE lending. Financial intermediaries incur high operating costs as they move down-market. The lending interest rate cap imposed may contribute to unfair competition against RCCs and may prevent them from serving otherwise bankable micro and small borrowers. The effect of Supreme Court rulings concerning usury has discouraged the formal sector from lending to this group and forced the group to accept higher rates from the black market. Resolving the conflict is necessary to increasing access.

49. The government should improve measurement of financial inclusion to allow meaningful performance monitoring and evaluation and to guide public policies. Using lending by county-level FIs as the criteria for agriculture related loan statistics is misleading and likewise, the definition of SMEs in China includes bigger companies than the intended small clients. Consideration should be given to designing a statistical system in keeping with international practice to lay emphasis on true outreach (measured by the number of micro loans and clients), efficiency, and financial sustainability.

VII. Financial Markets and Market Infrastructure

A. Financial Stability and Crisis Management

50. A review of the regulatory architecture is needed to ensure it is suited to the challenges posed by a rapidly evolving financial sector. China has adopted an institutional approach to financial regulation, with three separate commissions and the PBC sharing responsibilities (Table 7). The State Council has the overarching responsibility for the financial system. It exercised this responsibility by establishing and chairing a high-level ad-hoc committee of the key financial agencies in June 2008. The mission recommended that a permanent Financial Stability Committee be established, building on the experience from the ad-hoc committee.

51. China's crisis management arrangements fall under the purview of the State Council. The preference for responding to episodes of financial distress thus far has been with "open resolution" outcomes. This could have been influenced by Government's dual role in crisis management and ownership of institutions. As a result, injections of equity to undercapitalized banks and the de-risking of balance sheets through transfers of poorly performing assets to AMCs[5] has taken place starting in 1999.

52. Consideration should be given to establishing institutional arrangements and expanding the resolution toolkit so that closed resolution is a viable option for dealing with all banks. This should include providing supervisors with legal authority to intervene promptly in nonviable financial institutions; and providing a separate entity with the resources to close, recapitalize or sell such an institution and capacity to manage the intervened institution, including its assets. The authorities have given considerable thought to the introduction of a deposit insurance scheme and should accelerate this work, consistent with the large number of depository institutions and the need to reduce the financial exposure.

B. Money, Foreign Exchange, and Interbank Markets

53. The managed interest rate regime and exchange rate system has inhibited financial development and innovation. Continued advances in market based interest rate reform and improvements to the RMB exchange rate regime will improve financial development and innovation. Wholesale interest rates and derivative prices are unregulated. Although progress has been made in improving exchange rate flexibility since 2005, intraday movements of the exchange rate of RMB against the U.S. dollar in the inter-

---

[5] A strategy for AMCs established to help restructure banks needs to be developed. Transforming AMCs into commercial entities is recommended to eliminate moral hazard and to encourage banks to undertake quality risk analysis. In the interim, AMCs should be required to make periodic financial statements and management reports public.

bank spot market are limited to ±0.5 percent, and inter-day movements in the central parity rate have, in effect, not moved more than this, while retail interest rates remain regulated. Both limit the exchange rate and interest rate risk exposure of financials and corporates, thereby reducing the demand for hedging products and the incentive for financial market and product innovation. The PBC is actively researching and guiding innovation of financial institutions on tools to hedge FX risks.

54. Bond market efficiency would be enhanced by pursuing more active Government's issuance strategy, continuing to reform the interest rate regime, and addressing other price distortions. The issuance strategy could also be used as an instrument to foster secondary market liquidity. Arbitrage opportunities remain along different segments of the yield curve.

C. Systemic Liquidity

55. Abundant liquidity limits the risk of a systemic liquidity crisis in the near term, but complicates aggregate liquidity management. PBC's aggregate liquidity management would benefit from a move towards more indirect instruments. The PBC's control of base money is becoming difficult as capital controls become more challenging, financial markets develop, and China's integration in the global financial system proceeds. This argues for moving towards greater use of indirect instruments which could be tested in a pilot program to target a short-term money market interest rate.

56. Lowering reserve requirements and introducing reserve averaging would facilitate institutional level liquidity management and enhance stability. Consideration should be given to piloting reserve averaging at institutions with a structural surplus of funds, as well as several of those with a persistent deficit. To limit the impact of the PBC's liquidity management activities on the yields of MOF's issuances, both institutions should strengthen coordination when issuing in the same maturity segments. Different models could be assessed (e.g. Mexico, Brazil) to develop a framework suitable for China. The challenge is to preserve PBC's autonomy to guide short-term interest rates in line with its monetary policy goals and to conduct sterilization operations when needed, while supporting the MOF's ongoing development of a sustainable liquid risk-free yield-curve. Also, access to the PBC's standing facilities should be made more automatic and transparent with moral hazard concerns dealt with through pricing.

D. Payment and Securities Settlements Systems

57. The PBC has carried out a comprehensive reform of the China National Payments System (CNPS). The backbone is the High Value Payment System (HVPS), which is a systemically important payment system (SIPS). The assessment of the HVPS concludes that it broadly observes the Core Principles for SIPS. However, there is room for improvement, in particular with regard to the legal framework and oversight arrangements. The authorities should ensure the legal framework gives full protection to payments, derivatives and securities settlement finality. Regarding oversight, the PBC should clarify its policy stance in payment system oversight and determine the scope, major policies and instruments of the function. A more proactive oversight by the PBC of the China Foreign Exchange Trade System (CFETS) is advisable.

58. The FSAP team's assessment of securities and derivatives settlements systems suggest broad compliance with international standards. Improvements however could be made in the following areas:

- *Bond market CCDC system:* legal foundation, pre-settlement and settlement risk, governance, transparency, regulation and oversight:

- *Stock exchanges SD&C systems:* ensuring further robustness of the CCP and transparency;

- *Commodities futures markets-SHFE system:* legal foundation, margin requirements, and transparency.

E. Legal and Regulatory Structure

59. The structure of the legal framework for the financial sector has developed largely on a piecemeal basis. The framework could benefit from a routine review for effectively identifying and changing rules. While much has been done to ensure effective rule making in the form of public exposure and broad based consultation and interventions by the NPC Standing Committee and the State Council in ensuring timely reforms, more can be done to ensure effective implementation by having feedback mechanisms. In this regard, a "stock-take" of the gaps, overlaps and lack of clarity in the laws governing the financial sector is necessary.

60. China could benefit from applying a more principle-based approach in the formulation and implementation of laws. The regulatory system is rule-based, and there is a lack of flexibility for financial intermediaries to apply the rules and still have confidence that they have fully complied with them. The result is a high cost of compliance. The rule-base approach to regulation may have been appropriate, but going forward, consideration should be given to making it more principle-based.

61. The legal framework for insolvency proceedings and creditors' rights should be reviewed to provide for efficient and effective exit mechanisms. Detailed laws concerning the insolvency of financial institutions have not been developed for some sectors. The legal framework for insolvencies can be improved in areas relating to threshold tests, treatment of future claims and rules for dealing with cross border insolvencies. In addition, Consumer protection should be strengthened by building capacity in the courts to enforce contracts, empowering consumer organizations to play an effective role, enhancing personal data and privacy protection and by requiring market practices and codes of conduct to be in place.

F. Accounting and Auditing[6]

62. Chinese commercial banks have adopted the new *Chinese Accounting Standards (CAS)*, which have achieved substantial convergence with the International Financial Reporting Standards (IFRS). First introduced in 2007 by the MOF, CAS include a basic standard and 38 specific Accounting Standards for Business Enterprises. The capacity of the auditing profession is uneven and attention will need to be given to ensuring the quality of financial statements of small financial institutions matches that of large ones. The standard auditor independence regulation and oversight of the profession need to be improved.

G. Market Integrity

63. China has made significant progress in implementing its anti-money laundering and combating the financing of terrorism (AML/CFT) system. In 2007 the Financial Action Task Force (FATF) mutual evaluation report found the system in China to be acceptable, but lacking in some areas. The AML/CFT legal regime has since been strengthened and China has submitted a number of follow up reports to FATF reporting progress in addressing identified deficiencies. Based upon the submissions, the FATF plenary has concluded that China's level of compliance with its standards is now essentially largely compliant. However, two shortcomings remain. First, Chinese law and practice provides limited ability for authorities or financial institutions to have access to the identity of beneficial owners of legal persons. Second, preventive measures have not been sufficiently extended to non-financial businesses and professions.

---

[6] See also the 2009 World Bank *Report on the Observance of Standards and Codes–Accounting and Auditing*.

Table 1. Key Recommendations

Recommendations	Priority	Time-Frame
Improving commercialization		
1. Continue to advance the process of interest rate and exchange rate reform while ensuring that appropriate credit risk management practices in financial institutions are in place.	High	MT
2. Clearly delineate the roles and functioning of policy financial institutions from commercial financial institutions.	Medium	MT
3. Transform the four Asset Management Companies (AMCs) into commercial entities, and, as a first step, require them to make public periodic financial statements and management reports.	Medium	MT
Increasing efficiency of the institutional, regulatory, and supervisory framework		
4. Empower the PBC and three supervisory commissions with focused mandates, operational autonomy and flexibility, increased resources and skilled personnel, and strengthen interagency coordination to meet the challenges of a rapidly evolving financial sector.	High	MT
5. Develop a framework for regulation and supervision of financial holding companies (FHCs), financial conglomerates, and informal financial firms. In the interim, acquisition of a regulated institution should be approved by the regulatory commissions that are responsible for the underlying financial institutions.	Medium	NT
6. Introduce a more forward-looking assessment of credit risk in the CBRC risk rating system and eliminate deviations from the capital framework for credit and market risk.	Medium	NT
7. Introduce a formal program whereby the CSRC conducts regular comprehensive on-site inspections of the exchanges to improve oversight.	Medium	MT
8. Introduce a risk-based capital (RBC) solvency regime for insurance firms with suitable transition period and restrict new businesses by insurance companies operating below the 100 percent solvency level.	Medium	NT
9. Develop explicit and clear regulation for facilitating the exit of insurance companies from the market via run off or portfolio transfers.	Medium	MT
10. Enact a payment system law to give full protection to payments, derivatives and securities settlement finality.	High	MT
11. Ensure that beneficial ownership and control information of legal persons is adequate, accurate, and readily accessible to competent authorities.	High	MT
12. Improve information sharing and coordination arrangements among the PBC and other agencies on anti-money laundering (AML) and other supervisory issues.	High	MT
Upgrading the framework for financial stability, systemic risk monitoring, systemic liquidity, and crisis management		
13. Establish a permanent committee of financial stability, with the PBC as its secretariat.	High	MT
14. Upgrade data collection on financial institutions including their leverage, contingent liabilities, off-balance-sheet positions, unregulated products, and cross-border and sectoral exposures.	Medium	NT
15. Build a macro prudential framework for measurement and management of systemic risks; this should include increasing the resources and capacity of the PBC and regulatory agencies to monitor financial stability and to carry out regular stress tests.	High	NT
16. Enhance the sterilization of structural liquidity through market-based instruments and manage systemic liquidity spillovers via indirect monetary policy instruments.	High	NT

Recommendations	Priority	Time-Frame
Upgrading the framework for financial stability, systemic risk monitoring, systemic liquidity, and crisis management		
17. Introduce reserve averaging to facilitate liquidity management and enhance stability and efficiency.	High	NT
18. Start targeting a short-term repo rate on a pilot basis, as a trial of indirect liquidity management, and commence daily open market operations.	High	NT
19. Ensure that PBC's standing facilities operate immediately and automatically, with specified collateral requirement identical across all domestically incorporated institutions.	Medium	NT
20. Introduce a deposit insurance scheme to assist in the orderly wind-down of financial institutions and to help clarify the contingent liability.	Medium	NT
Developing securities markets and redirecting savings to contractual and collective investment sectors		
21. Ensure regulations are consistent and clarify regulatory responsibilities to support fixed income market development.	Medium	MT
22. Continue to improve bond issuance strategies between MOF and the PBC to help improve the existing market-making across all maturities of the yield curve.	High	MT
23. Upgrade regulatory and operational repo market framework to increase market liquidity, enhance risk management and reinforce the money and bond market interest rate nexus.	Medium	NT
24. Ease the 40 percent of net assets limit applicable to corporation's market based debt issuance to expand direct funding capacity.	Medium	MT
25. Upgrade links between China Central Depository Trust & Clearing Co., Ltd (CCDC) and Securities Depository and Clearing Corporation Limited (SD&C) to enhance connectivity among Interbank Bond Market (IBBM), Shanghai Stock Exchange (SSE), and Shenzhen Stock Exchange (SZSE), support further development, and contribute to efficiency in all three markets.	Medium	MT
26. Consolidate the multi-pillar pension system, with emphasis on the funded component.	Medium	MT
Improving alternative financing channels and access		
27. Review existing government programs to determine their effectiveness in promoting rural and micro and small enterprise (MSE) finance and formulate an integrated and coherent rural and MSE finance strategy.	High	MT
28. Further reform the rural credit cooperatives (RCCs) to enhance their efficiency and sustainability as commercial providers of financial products and services.	Medium	MT
29. Complete the reform of the Postal Savings Bank of China (PSBC) by optimizing equity ownership, overhauling the bank to become a corporation, and building effective corporate governance.	Medium	MT

Notes: 1. NT (Near Term) means implementation completed within 3 years; MT (Medium Term) means implementation completed in 3–5 years.

2. The table has been revised since the delivery of the Aide Mémoire.

Table 2. China: Financial Sector Reforms

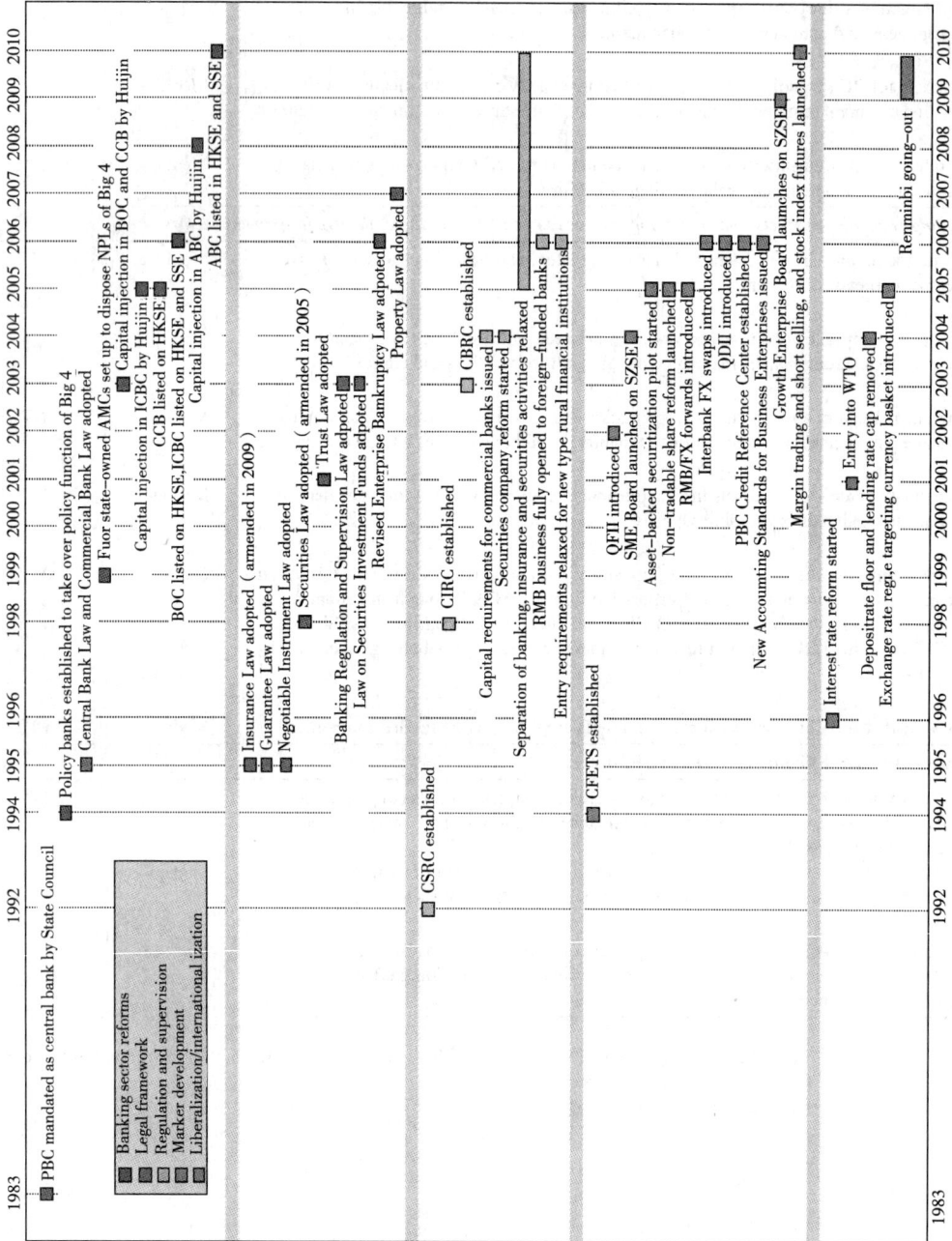

Legend:
- Banking sector reforms
- Legal framework
- Regulation and supervision
- Marker development
- Liberalization/international ization

Timeline axis: 1983 · 1992 · 1994 · 1995 · 1996 · 1998 · 1999 · 2000 · 2001 · 2002 · 2003 · 2004 · 2005 · 2006 · 2007 · 2008 · 2009 · 2010

Events:
- PBC mandated as central bank by State Council
- Policy banks established to take over policy function of Big 4
- Central Bank Law and Commercial Bank Law adopted
- Fuor state–owned AMCs set up to dispose NPLs of Big 4
- Capital injection in ICBC by Huijin
- Capital injection in BOC and CCB by Huijin
- CCB listed on HKSE
- BOC listed on HKSE,ICBC listed on HKSE and SSE
- Capital injection in ABC by Huijin
- ABC listed in HKSE and SSE
- Insurance Law adopted (amended in 2009)
- Guarantee Law adopted
- Negotiable Instrument Law adopted
- Securities Law adopted (armended in 2005)
- Trust Law adopted
- Banking Regulation and Supervision Law adopted
- Law on Securities Investment Funds adpoted
- Revised Enterprise Bamkruptcy Law adopted
- Property Law adopted
- CSRC established
- CIRC established
- CBRC established
- Capital requirements for commercial banks issued
- Securities company reform started
- Separation of banking, insurance and securities activities relaxed
- RMB business fully opened to foreign–funded banks
- Entry requirements relaxed for new type rural financial institutions
- CFETS established
- QFII introduced
- SME Board launched on SZSE
- Asset–backed securitization pilot started
- Non–tradable share reform launched
- RMB/FX forwards introduced
- Interbank FX swaps introduced
- QDII introduced
- PBC Credit Reference Center established
- New Accounting Standards for Business Enterprises issued
- Growth Enterprise Board launches on SZSE
- Margin trading and short selling, and stock index futures launched
- Interest rate reform started
- Entry into WTO
- Depositrate floor and lending rate cap removed
- Exchange rate regi,e targeting currency basket introduced
- Renminbi going–out

Note: The Big 4 banks are ICBC,CCB,ABC and BOC,which have been commercialized in recent years.The Big 4 and BOCOM together are referred to as large commercial banks.

Table 3. China: Selected Economic Indicators

	2005	2006	2007	2008	2009	2010
	(Annual percentage change, unless otherwise specified)					
National accounts and employment						
Real GDP	11.3	12.7	14.2	9.6	9.2	10.3
Consumption	8.1	9.8	11.1	8.6	8.4	8.1
Investment	10.6	13.6	14.7	11.0	20.8	12.0
Net exports[1]	2.6	2.0	2.5	0.8	-3.7	0.9
Consumer prices						
Average	1.8	1.5	4.8	5.9	-0.7	3.3
Unemployment rate (annual average)	4.2	4.1	4.0	4.2	4.3	4.1
	(In percent of GDP)					
External debt and balance of payments						
Current account	5.9	8.6	10.1	9.1	5.2	5.2
Trade balance	5.5	7.7	8.8	7.7	4.4	3.9
Capital and financial account	4.5	1.9	2.7	1.0	3.6	3.8
Gross external debt	13.1	12.5	11.1	8.6	8.6	9.3
Gross reserves	36.6	39.8	44.3	43.5	49.2	49.6
Saving and investment						
Gross domestic investment	42.1	43.0	41.7	44.0	48.2	48.8
National saving	49.2	51.6	51.9	53.2	53.5	54.0
Public sector finance						
General government gross debt	17.8	16.2	19.6	17.0	17.7	17.0
General government balance	-1.4	-0.7	0.9	-0.4	-3.1	-2.2
	(Annual percentage change)					
Real effective exchange rate	-0.5	1.6	4.0	9.2	3.3	-0.5

Sources: Data on net exports, external debt and balance of payments are provided by the Chinese authorities; the rest is based on historical data and staff estimates and projections.

1. Contribution to annual growth in percent.

Table 4. China: Structure of the Financial Sector, 2007–10

	2007				2008				2009				2010			
	Number of Institutions	Total Assets (in bln RMB)	Share of Total Assets	Share of GDP	Number of Institutions	Total Assets (in bln RMB)	Share of Total Assets	Share of GDP	Number of Institutions	Total Assets (in bln RMB)	Share of Total Assets	Share of GDP	Number of Institutions	Total Assets (in bln RMB)	Share of Total Assets	Share of GDP
Banking Institutions	**8,721**	**51,627**	**84.1**	**194.2**	**5,578**	**61,982**	**87.8**	**197.4**	**3,767**	**77,978**	**87.0**	**229.0**	**3,639**	**93,215**	**87.6**	**234.2**
Commercial banks	187	40,459	65.9	152.2	323	47,819	67.8	152.3	336	61,513	68.6	180.7	379	74,160	69.7	186.3
Large commercial banks	5	28,007	45.6	105.4	5	32,575	46.2	103.7	5	40,800	45.5	119.8	5	46,894	44.1	117.8
Joint-stock commercial banks	12	7,249	11.8	27.3	12	8,834	12.5	28.1	12	11,818	13.2	34.7	12	14,904	14.0	37.4
City commercial banks	124	3,340	5.4	12.6	136	4,136	5.9	13.2	143	5,680	6.3	16.7	147	7,853	7.4	19.7
Rural commercial banks	17	610	1.0	2.3	22	929	1.3	3.0	43	1,866	2.1	5.5	85	2,767	2.6	7.0
Foreign banks	29	1,252	2.0	4.7	148	1,345	1.9	4.3	133	1,349	1.5	4.0	130	1,742	1.6	4.4
Locally incorporated foreign subsidiaries	...	...	...	...	32	996	1.4	3.2	38	1,132	1.3	3.3	40	1,522	1.4	3.8
Branches of foreign banks	...	...	...	...	116	349	0.5	1.1	95	217	0.2	0.6	90	220	0.2	0.6
Policy banks and China Development Bank	3	4,278	7.0	16.1	3	5,645	8.0	18.0	3	6,946	7.7	20.4	3	7,652	7.2	19.2
China Postal Savings Bank	1	1,769	2.9	6.7	1	2,216	3.1	7.1	1	2,705	3.0	7.9	1	3,397	3.2	8.5

	2007				2008				2009				2010			
	Number of Institutions	Total Assets (in bln RMB)	Share of Total Assets	Share of GDP	Number of Institutions	Total Assets (in bln RMB)	Share of Total Assets	Share of GDP	Number of Institutions	Total Assets (in bln RMB)	Share of Total Assets	Share of GDP	Number of Institutions	Total Assets (in bln RMB)	Share of Total Assets	Share of GDP
Cooperative financial institutions	8,503	5,121	8.3	19.3	5,150	6,295	8.9	20.0	3,263	6,789	7.6	19.9	2,870	7,893	7.4	19.8
Rural cooperative banks	113	646	1.1	2.4	163	1,003	1.4	3.2	196	1,270	1.4	3.7	223	1,500	1.4	3.8
Urban credit cooperatives[1/]	42	131	0.2	0.5	22	80	0.1	0.3	11	27	0.0	0.1	1	2	0.0	0.0
Rural credit cooperatives[1/]	8,348	4,343	7.1	16.3	4,965	5,211	7.4	16.6	3,056	5,493	6.1	16.1	2,646	6,391	6.0	16.1
New-type rural financial institutions	27	0	0	0	101	6	0	0	164	25	0	0.1	386	113	0	0.3
Village or township banks	19	0	0	0	91	6	0	0	148	25	0	0.1	349	113	0	0.3
Rural mutual credit cooperatives	8	0	0	0	10	0	0	0	16	0	0	0	37	0	0	0
Non-Bank Financial Institutions	**690**	**9,744**	**15.9**	**36.7**	**738**	**8,582**	**12.2**	**27.3**	**772**	**11,666**	**13.0**	**34.3**	**782**	**13,168**	**12.4**	**33.1**
Insurance companies	102	2,831	4.6	10.6	112	3,280	4.6	10.4	120	3,971	4.4	11.7	125	4,965	4.7	12.5
Life	54	2,351	3.8	8.8	56	2,713	3.8	8.6	59	3,366	3.8	9.9	61	4,267	4.0	10.7
Re-insurance[1/]	6	89	0.1	0.3	9	101	0.1	0.3	9	116	0.1	0.3	9	115	0.1	0.3
Non-life	42	391	0.6	1.5	47	466	0.7	1.5	52	489	0.5	1.4	55	584	0.5	1.5
Pension funds	39	592	1.0	2.2	39	754	1.1	2.4	39	1,030	1.1	3.0	1	1,138	1.1	2.9
National Social Security Fund	1	440	0.7	1.7	1	562	0.8	1.8	1	777	0.9	2.3	1	857	0.8	2.2

Cont

	2007				2008				2009				2010			
	Number of Institutions	Total Assets (in bln RMB)	Share of Total Assets	Share of GDP	Number of Institutions	Total Assets (in bln RMB)	Share of Total Assets	Share of GDP	Number of Institutions	Total Assets (in bln RMB)	Share of Total Assets	Share of GDP	Number of Institutions	Total Assets (in bln RMB)	Share of Total Assets	Share of GDP
Enterprise annuities	38	152	0.2	0.6	38	191	0.3	0.6	38	253	0.3	0.7	...	281	0.3	0.7
Fund management companies	59	3,280	5.3	12.3	61	1,939	2.7	6.2	60	2,677	3.0	7.9	63	2,520	2.4	6.3
Securities investment funds[2]	346	3,280	5.3	12.3	439	1,939	2.7	6.2	577	2,677	3.0	7.9	704	2,520	2.4	6.3
Securities firms	106	1,734	2.8	6.5	107	1,191	1.7	3.8	106	2,027	2.3	6.0	106	1,967	1.8	4.9
Futures companies	177	50	0.1	0.2	171	59	0.1	0.2	167	121	0.1	0.4	164	192	0.2	0.5
Qualified Foreign Institutional Investors	51	286	0.5	1.1	76	179	0.3	0.6	94	290	0.3	0.9	106	297	0.3	0.7
Other non-bank financial institutions	152	972	1.6	3.7	168	1,181	1.7	3.8	182	1,550	1.7	4.6	213	2,089	2.0	5.2
Finance companies of enterprise groups	73	...	...	...	84	975	1.4	3.1	91	1,229	1.4	3.6	107	1,541	1.4	3.9
Trust companies	54	...	...	...	54	87	0.1	0.3	58	113	0.1	0.3	63	148	0.1	0.4
Finance leasing companies	10	...	...	...	12	80	0.1	0.3	12	160	0.2	0.5	17	316	0.3	0.8
Money brokerage firms	2	...	...	...	3	0.1	0.0	0.0	3	0.2	0.0	0.0	4	0.3	0.0	0.0
Finance companies	13	...	...	...	15	38	0.1	0.1	18	48	0.1	0.1	22	84	0.1	0.2
Lending companies	4	...	...	...	6	0	0	0	8	0	0	0	9	0.1	0	0

Cont

	2007				2008				2009				2010			
	Number of Institutions	Total Assets (in bln RMB)	Share of Total Assets	Share of GDP	Number of Institutions	Total Assets (in bln RMB)	Share of Total Assets	Share of GDP	Number of Institutions	Total Assets (in bln RMB)	Share of Total Assets	Share of GDP	Number of Institutions	Total Assets (in bln RMB)	Share of Total Assets	Share of GDP
Auto financing companies	9	...	...	...	9	38	0.1	0.1	10	48	0.1	0.1	13	84	0.1	0.2
Banking asset management companies[3]	4	...	...	...	4	...	...	...	4	...	...	...	4			
Total Financial System[4]	**9,411**	**61,370**	**100.0**	**230.9**	**6,316**	**70,564**	**100.0**	**224.7**	**4,539**	**89,644**	**100.0**	**263.3**	**4,421**	**106,383**	**100.0**	**267.3**

Sources: PBC, CBRC, CIRC, CSRC, NBS of China, and Ministry of Human Resource and Social Security.

1. As there is no insurance company engaged in both life and non-life business, data of reinsurance companies are provided instead. In 2007 the insurance sector adopted new accounting principles which are applied to the data starting from 2007.

2. Proceeds raised by securities investment funds are managed by fund management companies on behalf of fund unit holders.

3. The table excludes assets of the four AMCs. According to the FSAP team's calculations, the book value of the non-performing assets transferred to the AMCs amounted to about RMB2.6 trillion as of end 2006 (about 6 percent of total financial system assets or 12 percent of GDP). Comparable data for 2007–10 are not available, as the AMCs have not released financial statements since 2006.

4. This table does not include informal finance, the estimates of which vary.

Notes: Data for 2008–10 were provided by the Chinese authorities in the context of the FSAP. Data for 2007 were collected from publicly available sources, particularly the annual reports of the three financial regulatory agencies and the financial statements of the NSSF. Data on rural and urban credit cooperatives were collected from the CBRC's annual reports.

Table 5. China: Selected Indicators of Financial Health, 2005–10[1]

	2005	2006	2007	2008	2009	2010
				(In percent, unless otherwise indicated)		
Major Commercial Banks						
Capital Adequacy						
Regulatory capital to risk-weighted assets[2]	2.5	4.9	8.1	12.0	11.0	12.0
Regulatory Tier I capital to risk-weighted assets	...	...	6.0	9.6	8.5	9.6
Nonperforming loans net of provisions to capital	...	...	55.9	4.2	1.4	-2.2
Capital to assets[3]	4.3	5.2	5.4	5.9	5.3	6.0
Asset Quality						
Nonperforming loans to total gross loans	8.9	7.5	6.4	2.4	1.6	1.1
Loan loss provisions to non-performing loans[3]	24.8	34.3	39.2	117.9	155.4	217.7
Sectoral distribution of loans to total loans[4]						
Residents	...	...	97.8	97.9	99.3	...
Deposit takers	...	...	5.1	5.7	5.7	...
Central bank	...	...	3.0	2.1	4.2	...
Other financial corporations	...	...	1.0	1.7	1.1	...
General government	...	...	0.0	0.0	0.0	...
Non-financial corporations	...	...	70.5	69.8	68.3	...
Other domestic sectors	...	...	18.3	18.5	20.1	...
Non-residents	...	...	2.2	2.1	0.7	
Earnings and Profitability						
Return on assets[2]	0.6	0.9	1.4	1.4	1.4	1.5
Return on equity[2]	15.1	14.9	25.6	24.8	24.7	26.3
Interest margin to gross income[5]	...	...	83.6	81.1	78.0	79.1
Noninterest expenses to gross income[5]	...	...	41.2	37.0	38.4	35.5
Net interest margin[5]	2.5	2.4	2.8	2.9	2.3	2.5
Noninterest expenses to average assets[5]	1.7	1.7	1.6	1.8	1.4	1.4
Cost to income ratio[5]	46.3	51.7	39.2	38.1	41.7	36.8
Interest income to operating income[5]	87.4	90.2	87.7	87.1	84.8	84.2
Spread between reference lending and deposit rates[3]	333.0	360.0	333.0	306.0	306.0	306.0
Liquidity						
Liquid assets to total assets	...	...	22.1	23.5	22.8	22.6
Liquid assets to short-term liabilities	...	...	37.6	44.7	41.6	41.2
Exposure to foreign exchange risk						
Net open position in foreign exchange to capital	...	...	22.7	12.8	7.4	7.4
Non-Bank Sectors						
Insurance sector						
Coverage ratio[6]	...	...	444.0	210.0	223.0	206.0
Return on average equity (Life)	...	...	28.7	5.7	17.1	21.1
Return on average equity (Non-life)	...	...	-7.0	-26.2	2.9	21.5
State-owned enterprise corporate sector						
Number of SOEs[7]	127,067	119,254	115,087	113,731	115,115.0	...

	2005	2006	2007	2008	2009	2010
Total debt to equity ratio	1.7	1.7	1.4	1.4	1.6	...
Central government	1.4	1.4	1.2	1.3	1.4	...
Local government	2.4	2.3	1.9	1.8	1.9	...
Return on equity	5.6	6.2	7.2	8.7	5.7	...
Central government	8.3	8.6	10.4	6.8	7.0	...
Local government	2.2	3.2	6.4	4.4	4.3	...
Return on assets	2.0	2.1	3.0	3.6	2.2	...
Central government	3.2	3.2	4.8	3.0	3.0	...
Local government	0.6	0.9	2.2	1.5	1.5	...
Debt service coverage ratio[8]	4.12	4.43	7.25	3.72	4.3	...
Central government	6.55	6.96	7.41	4.36	5.0	...
Local government	2.83	3.33	4.30	2.94	3.4	...
Small- and medium-sized enterprises						
Number of SMEs[9]	242,061	269,031	300,262	385,721	393,074	...
Total debt to equity ratio	1.45	1.42	1.38	1.31	1.26	...
Return on assets	5.75	6.52	7.84	8.44	8.6	...
Return on equity	14.06	15.82	18.70	19.51	19.5	...
Debt service coverage ratio[8]	6.47	7.09	7.33	7.43	8.64	...
Real estate sector						
Commercial property inflation[10]	5.6	4.0	5.8	4.6	...	...
House price inflation[10]	8.4	6.4	8.2	7.1	...	...
Domestic residential house purchasing loans as percent of total loans[11]	...	...	...	12.5	14.0	14.5

Sources: PBC, MOF, CBRC, CIRC, State -Owned Asset Administration Commission, NBS of China, IMF Global Financial Stability Report, Bankscope, and IMF staff calculations.

1. All data for this table were provided by the Chinese financial regulatory and supervisory commissions in the context of the FSAP. The following footnotes describe some cases in which the figures were obtained from other publically available sources or calculated by the FSAP team.

2. Comparability across years is limited due to differences in data coverage. Data for 2005 and 2006 refer to the total banking industry as reported in the IMF Global Financial Stability Report, whereas data from 2008 to 2010 refer to the 17 major commercial banks as reported by the national authorities to the FSAP team.

3. Capital adequacy and asset quality indicators were calculated with data from CBRC's 2010 annual report. Capital to assets ratio is defined as equity to assets. Interest rate spreads were calculated with data from PBC's Monetary Policy Reports.

4. Ratios where the numerator and denominator were compiled on a domestically consolidated basis (DC).

5. Simple averages of 17 major commercial banks. FSAP team's calculations based on the banks' financial statements and Bankscope.

6. Available solvency margin over required solvency margin.

7. Number of non-financial SOEs above Grade Three. The State-Owned Assets Supervision and Administration Commission directly held SOEs are Grade One. Grade One SOEs directly held subsidiaries companies are Grade Two. Grade Two enterprises directly held subsidiaries are Grade Three.

8. Earnings before interest and tax as a percentage of interest and principal expenses.

9. Number of SMEs in the industrial sector.

10. Percent change in commercial real estate and house price indices.

11. CBRC's statistics based on credit data based on institution (legal person).

Table 6. China: Financial Development Indicators, 2005–10

	2005	2006	2007	2008	2009	2010
Banking						
Total number of banking institutions	-	19,667	8,721	5,578	3,767	3,639
Number of branches/million population	-	140	144	146	145	146
Bank deposits/GDP (%)	147.2	153.3	143.5	147.5	169.6	171.3
Private credit[1]/GDP (%)	114.3	113.0	111.0	108.3	129.3	131.1
Bank assets/total financial system assets (%)	-	-	84.1	87.8	87.0	87.6
Bank assets/GDP (%)	197.1	198.3	194.2	197.4	229.0	234.2
Insurance						
Number of life insurers	42	48	54	56	59	61
Number of non-life insurers	35	38	42	47	52	55
Insurance Penetration (premiums in % of GDP)						
Life	1.8	1.7	1.8	2.2	2.3	-
Non-life	0.9	1.0	1.1	1.0	1.1	-
Insurance Density (premiums per capita, RMB)						
Life	250	272	336	498	554	-
Non-life	129	155	194	234	273	-
Pension						
Percentage of labor force covered by pensions	30.1	31.5	32.8	35.4	41.2	45.7[2]
Pension fund assets/GDP (%)	1.5	1.7	2.2	2.4	3.0	2.9
Pension fund assets/total financial system assets (%)	-	-	-	1.1	1.1	1.1
Mortgage						
Mortgage assets/total financial system assets (%)	-	-	-	4.2	5.0	5.2
Mortgage debt stock/GDP (%)	-	-	-	9.4	13.1	14.0
Money markets						
Interbank lending (RMB billion)	1,278	2,150	10,647	15,049	19,350	27,868
Pledged repo value of transactions (RMB billion)	15,678	26,302	44,067	56,383	67,701	84,653
Outright repo value of transactions (RMB billion)	219	292	726	1,758	2,602	2,940
Central bank bill value traded (RMB billion)	2,893	4,240	8,704	22,827	14,213	17,465
Foreign exchange markets						
Foreign exchange reserves in months of imports	13.3	14.4	16.8	18.1	24.6	-
Foreign exchange reserves/short-term debt	4.8	5.4	6.5	8.6	9.3	7.6
Value of transactions in FX swap (USD billion)	0	51	315	441	806	1,296
Value of transactions in FX forward (USD billion)	2.7	14.1	22.6	17.9	11.7	36.4
Capital Markets						
Equity market						
Number of listed companies	1,387	1,440	1,550	1,625	1,700	2,063
Market capitalization of listed companies[3]/GDP (%)	17.5	41.3	123.1	38.6	71.6	66.7
Stock market value traded/market capitalization[3] (%)	96.4	100.4	140.8	220.1	219.7	205.6
Number of new offers	15	66	124	76	99	347
Value of new offers (RMB billion)	5.8	134.2	481.0	103.4	187.9	488.3

	2005	2006	2007	2008	2009	2010
Bond market						
Government bonds outstanding[4]/GDP (%)	27.3	28.9	32.4	31.3	29.3	28.1
Financial bonds outstanding/GDP (%)	10.8	12.1	12.7	13.4	15.1	15.0
Corporate bonds outstanding/GDP (%)	1.7	2.6	3.0	4.1	7.1	8.6
Derivatives market						
Total market value of warrants traded on SSE and SZSE (RMB billion)	-	-	54.0	17.5	20.9	1.5
Annual turnover of warrants on SSE and SZSE (RMB billion)	-	-	7,783	6,969	5,365	1,499
Annual turnover of commodity futures (RMB trillion)	-	-	20.5	36.0	65.3	113.5
Total notional outstanding of RMB interest rate derivatives5 (RMB billion)	5.0	33.3	217	529	662	1,486
Average daily trading volume of RMB interest rate derivatives (RMB billion)	0.0	0.1	0.9	2.1	1.9	6.0
Collective investment funds						
Number of licensed investment funds	-	-	346	439	557	704
Number of fund management companies	-	-	59	61	60	63
Total assets under management by investment funds/GDP (%)	-	-	12.3	6.2	7.9	6.3
Share of retail investors in investment funds (%)	-	-	89	81	82	82
Memo:						
Nominal GDP (RMB billion)	18,494	21,631	26,581	31,405	34,051	39,798
Population (million)	1,304	1,311	1,318	1,325	1,331	1,338

Source: PBC, CBRC, CIRC, CSRC, MOHRSS, CFETS, BIS, IFS, WDI, and Swiss Re Sigma and ChinaBond.com.cn.
Notes: 1. Including credit to public enterprises.
      2. Labor force data for 2010 is an estimate.
      3. Including all the A and B shares of companies listed on SSE and SZSE.
      4. Data for government bonds are from the BIS and include both treasury securities and central bank bills/notes.
      5. Estimates by CFETS.

Table 7. China: Financial System Architecture

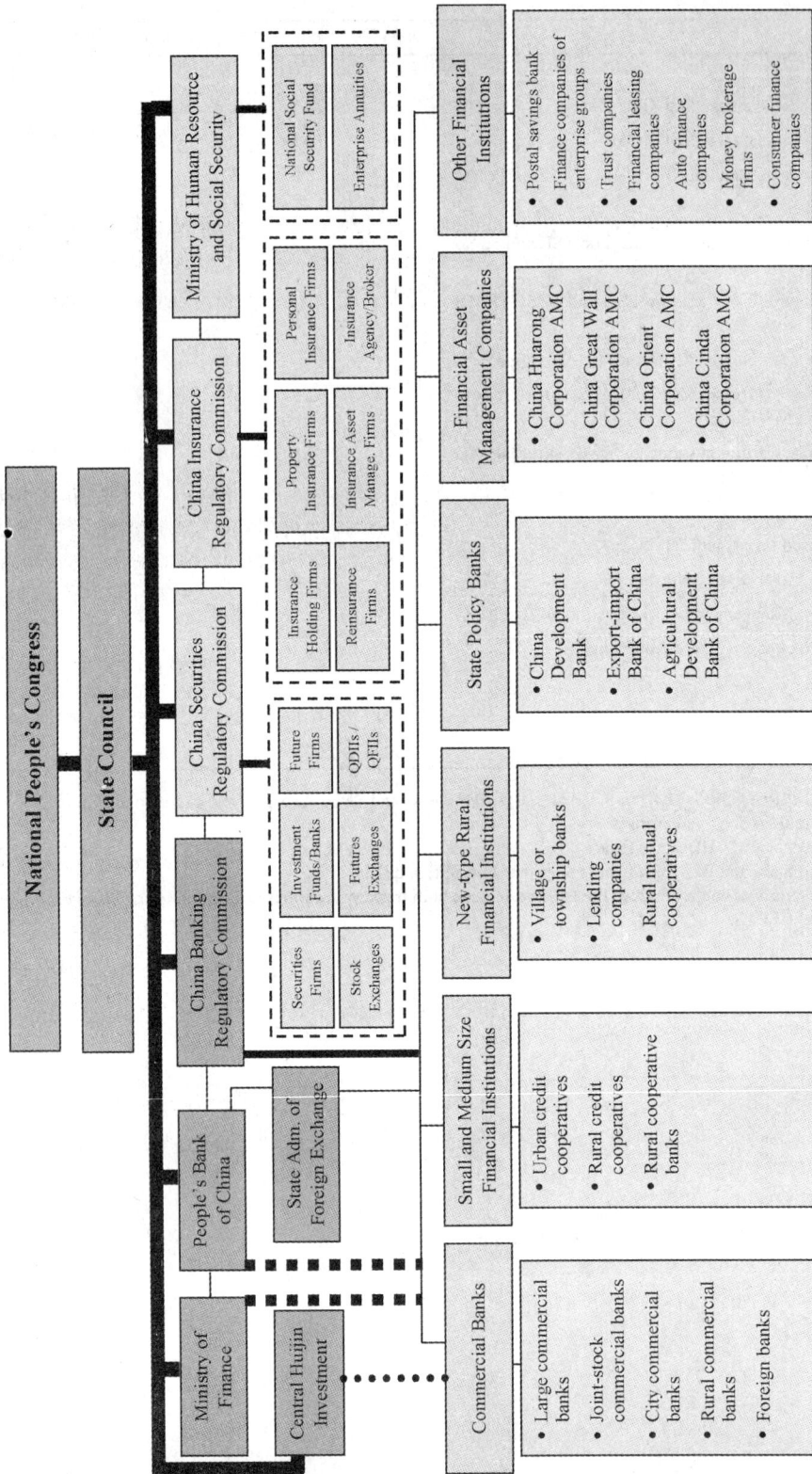

National People's Congress

State Council

Ministry of Finance — Central Huijin Investment — People's Bank of China — State Adm. of Foreign Exchange — China Banking Regulatory Commission — China Securities Regulatory Commission — China Insurance Regulatory Commission — Ministry of Human Resource and Social Security

China Banking Regulatory Commission
- Securities Firms
- Stock Exchanges
- Investment Funds/Banks
- Futures Exchanges
- Future Firms
- QDIIs/QFIIs

China Securities Regulatory Commission
- Insurance Holding Firms
- Reinsurance Firms
- Property Insurance Firms
- Insurance Asset Manage. Firms
- Personal Insurance Firms
- Insurance Agency/Broker

Ministry of Human Resource and Social Security
- National Social Security Fund
- Enterprise Annuities

Commercial Banks
- Large commercial banks
- Joint-stock commercial banks
- City commercial banks
- Rural commercial banks
- Foreign banks

Small and Medium Size Financial Institutions
- Urban credit cooperatives
- Rural credit cooperatives
- Rural cooperative banks

New-type Rural Financial Institutions
- Village or township banks
- Lending companies
- Rural mutual cooperatives

State Policy Banks
- China Development Bank
- Export-import Bank of China
- Agricultural Development Bank of China

Financial Asset Management Companies
- China Huarong Corporation AMC
- China Great Wall Corporation AMC
- China Orient Corporation AMC
- China Cinda Corporation AMC

Other Financial Institutions
- Postal savings bank
- Finance companies of enterprise groups
- Trust companies
- Financial leasing companies
- Auto finance companies
- Money brokerage firms
- Consumer finance companies

Notes: The thickest connectiong lines correspond to the highest leves of authority in financial policy making. The NPC promulgates all financial sector laws and the State Council executes financial regulation and issues mandatory policy directives to all the financial regulatory and supervisory agencies. The dotted connecting lines indicate the three primary functions of PBC —formulating monetary policy, maintaining financial stability, and providing financial services— and the triple role of the MOF as tax administrator, treasurer, and owner of several commercial banks. The thinner connecting lines emerging from CBRC, CSRC, CIRC, and MHRSS reflect that these entities are mostly responsible for regulating and conducting and oversight of their resective financial sectors.

Additional notes: The SAFE is responsible for foreign exchange operations of securities and insurance companies. The China Development Bank and the Postal Savings Bank are in the process of reforming into commercial banks. Central Huijin exercise rights and obligations as an investor in major state-owned financial enterprises on behalf of the State. The National Social Security Fund has also a dual role as an institutional investor and a stakeholder in some of the largest commercial banks.